This book is dedicated to Michael J. Reynolds.
Without his help and support none of this would have been possible.

The Saxonia Sisters

The Story Of Four Splendid Liners

by
Clive Harvey

Published by
Carmania Press
Unit 212, Station House, 49, Greenwich High Road, London, SE10 8JL, Great Britain.

ISBN 0 9534291 9 9   First published 2001.
British Library Cataloguing for Publication Data.
A Catalogue Record for this book is available from the British Library.

Artwork production by Alan Kittridge.
Printed by The Amadeus Press, Ltd., Cleckheaton, West Yorkshire.

Contents

FRONT COVER: Sisters in their prime: An evocative Stephen Card painting of *Carinthia* at New York with the *Franconia* in cruising green, manoeuvring in the background. *Stephen J. Card.*

BACK COVER: *Franconia* cruising to the sun. *Captain Ron Warwick collection.*

FRONTICE: A brave display. *Captain Ron Warwick collection.*

BACK COVER: *Franconia* in her heyday. *Captain Ron Warwick collection.*

Introduction

In the 1950s, even if you lived hundreds of miles from Southampton or Liverpool as I did, everyone knew that if you wanted to go to America you sailed Cunard. The aeroplane just did not come into the equation at all. Thus, in my childhood the mighty 'Queens', *Queen Elizabeth* and *Queen Mary*, were in their heyday and really were 'the only way to cross' – even if we did have an idea that the *United States* might actually be more exciting! Then, when I was about 9 years old, I discovered the Cunard liner *Saxonia*.

I had been given a copy of The Observer's Book of Ships – a volume with an awful lot of uninspiring profile drawings. However, to the delight of my young eyes, there were the glossy coloured pages in the centre of the book. Among the signal and national flags, the funnel markings, the tankers, fishing boats and naval vessels, was a selection of ocean liners: *Edinburgh Castle, Iberia, Antilles, United States* and ... *Saxonia*. There she was, sailing proudly under the Jacques Cartier Bridge – it was love at first sight!

By the mid-1960s, when I had left school, I discovered the delights of haunting the travel agency offices for brochures and deck plans of ocean liners. Even in those days, it was still possible to book a liner voyage to almost anywhere in the World – albeit that the moment to do so was fading fast. Among my horde of brochures were some on *Carmania* and *Franconia* – *Saxonia* and her sister *Ivernia* rebuilt into cruise ships. The elegance! The style! The glamour! To my eyes they were the ultimate ocean liners!

It would be almost ten years before I would actually see one of the Saxonia sisters and that would be none other than the former *Saxonia* herself. By this time, however, she was no longer an elegant Cunard liner but the somewhat down-graded *Leonid Sobinov* – pride of the Soviet Russian fleet. Glimpsing her from the terminal building as we waited to board, however, I could not see the 'hammer and sickle' device on her funnel. Once on board, I could ignore the faded furniture and the chipped bases to the table lamps and then it all looked just as it had done in those brochures. After all, the coat hangers in the wardrobe were still stamped 'Cunard Line'. It was a midnight sailing and, as we slipped from our berth, we passed *Canberra, Windsor Castle* and *Northern Star*. It was so easy to believe that at last I was sailing on board the fabulous *Carmania*, ex-*Saxonia*.

Later years would find me aboard two of her sisters: *Sylvania* and *Carinthia*, but as *Dawn Princess* and *Fair Princess*. Through the Mediterranean on *Dawn Princess*; at anchor off Monte Carlo or making a stately arrival in Venice; sailing under Sydney Harbour Bridge aboard *Fair Princess* and seeing her serenely at anchor off some palm-fringed South Pacific island. Both of those lovely ships generated wonderful memories and allowed me to create those images of the ships in locations far more exotic than the first picture of *Saxonia* passing under the Jacques Cartier Bridge. However, it was that midnight sailing, passing some of the finest British ocean liners while aboard 'my' *Saxonia/Carmania*, that was the most magical moment of all.

Clive Harvey.
January, 2001.

Foreword

By William H. Miller

The *Saxonia* and her three sisters, the *Ivernia*, the *Carinthia* and the *Sylvania*, were among my favourite ships. They were the new and trendy Cunarders of the 1950s, to an extent smaller versions of the *Caronia* of 1948. The new ships had one mast placed above the wheelhouse, a single but domed stack and a nicely raked bow. They also had what was something of a Cunard trademark: the cruiser stern. We thought of them as ocean liners but, with no less than eight kingposts and sixteen booms, they were actually more like big combination passenger-cargo ships.

Following the debut of the last of them, the *Sylvania*, in June 1957, the great Cunard company – the biggest passenger ship operator on the still very lucrative North Atlantic – did not add another liner to its fleet until the *Queen Elizabeth 2* in May 1969, a space of a dozen years. In the interim, there was the great withering: the arrival of jet crossings in October 1958 and then the quick, merciless decline of the Cunard and almost all other Atlantic passenger fleets in the 1960s. The *Saxonia* and the *Ivernia* served Cunard for nearly twenty years, the *Carinthia* and *Sylvania* for over ten. Each ship went on to other, very interesting careers and, rather amazingly, three remain afloat to this day. They are very deserving ships: deserving of their own book. I wish I had written it myself. Instead, great praises and warmest congratulations to Clive Harvey, a friend, a World-class cruise traveller and a grand-class ocean liner historian, for preparing this splendid work on the careers of this Cunard foursome.

I have some remembrances of my own of these ships. They were familiar sights to me in the later 1950s, coming and going in New York during the Atlantic winter season, from December through April, when the St. Lawrence and therefore the intended Canadian service was closed. They had especially long layovers in those days – arriving, for example, on Saturday mornings and then sailing again five or six days later, on a Thursday or Friday, usually at 10.30 in the morning. I often wanted to skip school just to see one of them heading out. Once, but on a midnight sailing, I visited the *Carinthia* and I recall seeing the *Aquitania*'s chairs now being re-used in the First Class restaurant. I also recall visiting the *Franconia*, refitted from *Ivernia*, as she prepared to sail on a Christmas trip to the Caribbean in December 1963. She had been modernized, rebuilt aft and was now painted Cunard's 'cruising green', matching the likes of the celebrated *Caronia* and the second *Mauretania*. The *Franconia* later became something of a fixture in New York harbour with her weekly Saturday sailings to Bermuda, a successor to the old Furness-Bermuda Line. We often went aboard, acted like the 'real' passengers and sipped thirty-five cent cocktails.

I did a trip to Alaska from San Francisco in July 1976 on Sitmar Cruises' totally rebuilt *Fairsea*, the former *Carinthia*. There were few obvious traces, at least in the passenger quarters, of her old Cunard days by then. By the 1990s, I recall being turned away from the *Feodor Shalyapin*, ex-*Franconia*, ex-*Ivernia*, at Naples by a sympathetic crewman, who was embarrassed by the sorry condition of "my country's ship". He did offer, though, to sell me some rusted tools and empty wine bottles. On another occasion (in August 1994), I remember, during a stop over at Valletta on Malta, seeing both the *Shalyapin* and her sister, the *Leonid Sobinov*, the onetime *Saxonia*, in port together. They looked almost identical in adjoining berths, but had different funnel colours and markings by then.

Most recently, in the fading light of an October afternoon, I saw the *Albatros*, the former *Sylvania*, heading out of the Hudson. She had come to New York on a long cruise with mostly German passengers and had a two-night stay for the convenience of her guests. She had actually used one of the former Cunard berths up at West 50th Street. But few probably noticed either the ship or the pier she used. To New York harbor watchers, her visit was perhaps a last link to Clive's Saxonia Sisters. But happily, they live on in his glorious book.

The whistles are sounding! Let's start a wonderful, informative and enlightening read about four fascinating passenger ships: *Saxonia, Ivernia, Carinthia* and *Sylvania.*

William H. Miller,
Secaucus, New Jersey.
February, 2001.

The Saxonia Sisters

Streaked with rust and careworn from several years of neglect, the proud old liner, still dignified in her decay, slowly made her way under the care of tugs. In the shimmering heat of an Indian day, she headed towards Alang to await her destruction. Her distinctly domed funnel, high, almost flat-fronted bridge structure and enclosed promenade all indicated that she had been a liner built, not for the searing heat of India, but for the grey and cold North Atlantic. While the name on her rust-streaked bow was most certainly of Russian origin, *Leonid Sobinov*, she had been better known as the Cunard liner *Saxonia*. She was the lead ship of the long-lived quartet of 'Saxonia Sisters'.

The entry into service, in June 1957, of the twin-screw passenger and cargo liner *Sylvania* marked the completion of a 90,000-ton building programme undertaken by John Brown & Co. (Clydebank), Ltd. for the Cunard Steam Ship Co., Ltd. of Liverpool. Within three years, four magnificent liners – *Saxonia, Ivernia, Carinthia* and then *Sylvania* – had left the famous Clydebank yard to join Cunard's Canadian service. They had all been built to meet the requirements of Canada's rapidly growing population and increasing volume of overseas trade. The basic design of the ships combined a large passenger capacity, in maximum comfort, with space for a substantial amount of cargo – all within the biggest dimensions which would permit safe navigation of the St. Lawrence River up to the terminal port of Montreal.

Passenger figures for the sister ships during those early years gave every indication of long and profitable careers for the line. Speaking aboard the *Sylvania* while she was at Greenock on the eve of her maiden voyage in June 1957, Mr. Frank H. Dawson, director and general manager of the Cunard Line, revealed that the *Saxonia*, the first of the quartet, which had entered service in September 1954, had already carried 58,500 passengers. The *Ivernia*, which had followed her into service in July 1955, had carried 43,200 and the *Carinthia*, whose maiden voyage had begun in June 1956, had carried 18,600. Mr. Dawson also mentioned that since 1947, Cunarders in the Canadian trade had carried 614,000 passengers across the Atlantic.

The association between the Cunard Line and Canada dated back to 1840. The tiny *Unicorn*, the first ship of the line to cross the Atlantic, and the *Britannia*, first of the mail steamers with which Samuel Cunard began his regular service between Europe and the New World, both steamed into Halifax, Nova Scotia during the summer of that year. Of course, going back even further, Samuel Cunard himself was Canadian, having been born in Halifax in 1787. The direct link between Britain and Canada which this visionary man created was maintained for over twenty

years. The service to Halifax was ended in the 1860s, Cunard liners then going directly to Boston or to New York. However, their superior speed and great reputation ensured that the line continued to draw large numbers of passengers travelling between Europe and Canada.

In 1911, the company re-entered the Canadian trade, acquiring the Thomson Line and their three ships. They were re-named *Albania, Ausonia* and *Ascania. Albania* was less than successful, not really being up to the standard of other Cunard ships and, after six months, she was laid up and offered for sale. The other two, though far from ideal, were rather more successful but sadly were lost during the First World War. Realising that the former Thomson Line ships did not meet their required standard, Cunard ordered a pair of purpose-built liners for the Canadian service, from Scotts' Shipbuilding & Engineering Co. of Greenock, in the early days of 1912. They were to become the *Andania* and *Alaunia*. A third ship of the class, *Aurania*, was ordered in December, 1913 from Swan, Hunter & Wigham Richardson. Unfortunately, these three new ships were also lost to enemy action during the war.

By 1921, three new ships had been launched for the Canadian service. These were the *Antonia, Ausonia* (II) and *Andania* (II) and were the first in what was to become a fleet of six very similar 14,000-ton liners. The remaining three ships, *Aurania* (II), *Ascania* (II) and *Alaunia* (II), all entered service in 1924-25 and during the remaining inter-war years these six liners became well known on both sides of the Atlantic. All were called to service during the Second World War and only the *Ascania* was returned to the company, even then not until 1947. After a very brief refit, she was assigned the task of re-establishing the company's normal passenger services to Canada. Her first sailing on this revived route from Liverpool began in December of that year. She maintained the service until 1955.

A new phase of Cunard association with Canada had begun, however, in July 1946 when the *Aquitania* made a single voyage to Halifax. Actually, it was not until the 1st April, 1948 that she was officially handed back to Cunard. After a brief overhaul, she was placed on charter to the Canadian government for a series of 11 voyages between Southampton and Halifax and she sailed on the first of these on the 25th May. The charter was renewed for a further 14 voyages the following year and at this time the ship carried many Canadian servicemen and their British wives and children who were beginning new lives in Canada. *Aquitania* ended her final Canadian voyage when she arrived back at Southampton on the 1st December, 1949. She was then sold for scrap in early 1950, having had the distinction of being the last remaining four-funnelled liner.

Following their release from war service, the *Scythia, Samaria* and *Franconia* also carried thousands of settlers to Canada. These pre-War liners and the excitingly new *Saxonia* were supported in the Canadian service by five fast cargo liners, *Asia, Arabia, Assyria, Andria* and *Alsatia*, the latter two having been acquired from the Silver Line and re-named.

In the final weeks of 1951, Cunard announced that they had decided to build a completely new class of ships for the service between Liverpool and Montreal. This initial announcement only mentioned two ships , though this was soon extended to include two further vessels. They were to be the largest Cunard liners ever built purely for the company's Canadian service. They were, however, quoted in the annoucement as being of 22,000 gross tons, quite an average size compared to the rest of the ships in the fleet. While initially all indications were good, by the time the third and fourth liners were under construction it had become obvious that the pattern of transportation was about to undergo a radical change. Even while the first two, the *Saxonia* and *Ivernia*, were being built, plans were being laid by some airlines to introduce the trans-continental jet airplane. Nevertheless, the Cunard directors remained convinced for another decade that there would always remain enough people who would wish to travel in a certain degree of luxury and style to keep their fleet of transatlantic liners viable. Sadly, this was not to prove to be the case, but their blind faith has in the end provided us with four liners which have gone on to give sterling service to other owners and to bring travelling pleasure to many hundreds of thousands of passengers.

Saxonia

It had been announced on the 25th November, 1953, that the first two vessels of the class would be named *Saxonia* and *Ivernia*. This revived memories of the two ships that had carried those names earlier in the century. The previous *Saxonia* had also been built at Clydebank by John Brown & Co., Ltd., in 1900. A 14,000-ton vessel capable of carrying 1,500 passengers, she had first sailed on the Liverpool – Boston route, later being involved in a service from the Mediterranean to New York. She survived the First World War and remained in service for the line until being sold for scrap in 1925.

In January, 1954, Cunard announced that the second *Saxonia*, the lead ship in their new class, would be named the following month by Lady Churchill, the wife of the then Prime Minister. At the same time, it was stated that the sister ship, *Ivernia*, would be launched later in the year by Mme. St. Laurent, the wife of the Canadian Prime Minister. At noon on Wednesday, the 17th February, 1954, the new *Saxonia* slid down the ways to meet her natural environment and, despite the bad weather, winter sunshine illuminated the emblem of the rampant Cunard lion on her stem. *Saxonia* was the first modern Cunarder to

Ready for launching, *Saxonia* shows off the recess for the stern anchor required in the St. Lawrence.
Captain Ron Warwick collection.

The newly completed *Saxonia* in the Clyde. *Peter Kohler collection.*

revive memories of the figureheads and clipper bows of the past. She was then towed to the fitting out basin. Even prior to her launch, her handsome, clean, modern lines had been evident, while prominent on her stern was the special anchor for use in the St. Lawrence.

At the celebratory luncheon held shortly after Lady Churchill had performed the naming ceremony, she read a message from her husband which aptly summed up the purpose of the *Saxonia*: "Canada, as well as being a glorious member of the British Commonwealth of Nations, is also the link across the Atlantic Ocean of the English-speaking world. Here we are creating physical arrangements which help to turn into actual important facts those aims for an even closer unity to which we aspire." As a memento of the launching, Lady Churchill was presented with an 18th century diamond brooch.

Saxonia was at the time the largest Cunard liner to be built for the Canadian service; and it seemed as though growing population and an increasing volume of overseas trade had created a need for the right type of liner service to meet the demands of both. The directors believed that in *Saxonia* and her sisters they had found the appropriate combination. The *Saxonia* was to be fitted to carry 125 First Class and 800 Tourist Class passengers in the highest standard of comfort of the day. Equally important were her cargo-carrying facilities. There were six hatches which served five holds, two forward and three aft of the machinery spaces. Several of these hatches were flush to the deck, thereby increasing the available outdoor space for passengers to enjoy. There was also associated 'tweendeck space for the carriage of general cargo. The hatches and holds were served by handling gear designed to enable the ship to maintain a rapid turnround time, an essential factor for a liner on a strict passenger-carrying schedule. She had a cargo capacity of some 300,000 cubic feet, a figure that included 15,000 cubic feet of insulated space for the carriage of perishable goods.

In appearance, *Saxonia* was quite unlike any previous Cunard liner and it was her distinctive dome-topped funnel that gave her that very special silhouette. It was an aluminium structure, rising to 44 feet above deck level, and its design was based on a long series of wind tunnel tests intended to ensure that all smoke and exhaust gases would be dispersed well clear of the ship without causing problems anywhere on the open decks. The dome was pierced by four circular apertures through which were expelled the smoke and exhaust gases from the furnaces which heated the four main boilers. Handrails encircled the dome and enabled painting and maintenance work to be carried out. A great deal of thought had gone into the design of the new ship and consideration for the comfort of her passengers was paramount. Denny-Brown stabilisers were fitted, making her the very first Cunard Line ship to be given these anti-rolling devices at the time of her building.

It took nearly six months from her launching to complete *Saxonia*. On the 9th August, 1954 she left the fitting out berth for dry-docking, then sailed from Glasgow on the 18th for her trials. Finally, she arrived in Liverpool on the 23rd to prepare for her maiden voyage. As completed, she had a gross tonnage of 21,637, was 608 feet 3 inches in overall length and had a breadth of 80 feet. She had nine decks: Sports, Boat, Promenade, Main, "A", Restaurant, "B", "C" and "D". There was accommodation for 457 officers and crew, as well as that for her passengers.

Since she was designed principally for the Canadian service, it was only natural that Canadian themes should dominate the public rooms of the new liner. Her designers created some strikingly modern and original schemes, quite unlike those aboard any other ship of the line, and quite refreshing in their modernity for a British liner. The brief for her designers was that they should acknowledge several aspects of Canadian life and history: the races and countries which contributed to the making of the nation; its natural resources and wild life; and the colonising of the land. The arts and crafts of the native North Americans proved a rich storehouse of imaginative design and considerable research led to the adoption of many examples of tribal motifs in the decorative themes of the public rooms.

The discovery of the St. Lawrence River by Cartier in 1536 was reflected in three circular paintings by the Canadian artist Tom Luzny which were placed at the head of the Tourist forward staircase. The rugged, timbered effect produced in the Tourist Smoking Room recalled the early days of the British and other European settlers. In the First Class Cocktail Bar, the "Yukon Bar", the influence was gold – one of Canada's traditional resources with a picturesque history. The wild life of the country was reflected in more of Tom Luzny's works: a Beaver Dam mural on the Tourist aft staircase and another mural, this one of a grizzly bear climbing a tree in search of honey, was a feature of the Tourist Smoking Room.

The principal public rooms were on Promenade Deck and forward on the Boat Deck. There, with large windows facing out over the bow, was the First Class Lounge, the Chintz Lounge. The walls were decorated with delicate pink sheet plastic panels which were studded with painted mirror insets, each with a miniature flower design. The curtains were of a plain wine-coloured satin and the brown carpet had a swirling pattern that was derived from the whorls made by oil floating on water. This room was the social centre of the First Class accommodation and its central feature was a dance floor, separated from the forward seating area by a decorative balustrade. An orchestra platform was on the aft wall. The room was furnished with club chairs and matching sofas upholstered in a contemporary design in black, wine, yellow and grey. If the Canadian-themed décor was not apparent in this room, it was even less so in the First Class Smoking Room. Here the designers had looked back to traditional styles and had given the room a Regency character.

However, the Yukon Bar could hardly have been more different in its style. In fact, Cunard literature of the day described the look of the room as "robust.... recreating in sophisticated fashion a picturesque legend of Canadian history – the life and environment of the early gold prospectors." A more unlikely theme for the decoration of a cocktail bar it would be hard to find! There were more of Tom Luzny's murals, one showing prospectors panning for gold while another, perhaps more attractive, depicted the northern lights or aurora borealis. Gold-textured aluminium panelled the walls along with other panels that recreated the crystal shapes made by frost. The doors and shutters were black and red, in a bold pattern that was supposed to recall the check shirts worn by the miners. Various check patterns were also used for the seating.

The Canadian theme was also evident in the First Class Dining Saloon, known as the Maple Leaf Restaurant. This traditional emblem of Canada was used on the wall panels along with an unusual combination of other motifs associated with Canadian history: the fleur de lys, the tomahawk and the bow and arrow. A stylised maple leaf design was also incorporated in the design of the floor covering.

With 800 Tourist passengers aboard, it is not surprising that the Tourist Class Lounge was the largest public room on the ship. It was considered to be among the finest Tourist Class spaces on any Atlantic liner of the day. The windows on each side looked out to a broad glass-enclosed promenade, while a raised central dome above the large dance floor extended the room through two decks. The walls were covered in squared, woven glass fabric panels, flanked by other panels covered with reinforced plastic fabric. The textures and effects of these materials created a symmetry which was referred to as "atomic pattern" and in some instances recalled the crystal structure diagrams which the scientist prepares to record the way in which atoms are arranged. With such striking modernity, it was perhaps a relief to some that the green carpet was patterned with wild flowers. In fact, with green and beige armchairs, patterned with a design of seashells, the room appears to have been very attractive.

The North American theme was picked up again in the Tourist Smoking Room, otherwise known as the Choctaw Room. The bold, angular designs found on the tribal blankets of the Choctaw tribe were used in the décor. They were used to decorate the walls, between panels of Douglas fir. There were also twin totem poles and, adjoining the room, was a cocktail bar decorated in the same style. The Tourist Garden Lounge was very much a daytime area, its teak-framed furniture covered in webbing with a check of red and silver or green and silver. The garden aura was created by plants and flowers in green anodised aluminium boxes. Part of the Lounge led out through coloured, striped canopies to the promenade deck and this created a "street café" effect.

The Tourist Class Restaurant extended the whole width of the ship and seated almost 500 passengers. It was a simple and functional room with a colour scheme of grey and pink. It was known as the Odahmin Restaurant, odahmin being the native American name for the wild strawberry. Fabric with a design of this fruit was used in the blinds to cover the portholes that lined both sides of the room. The dining chairs were sycamore-framed with grey, pink or black seats and backs.

All the First Class cabins, which were either doubles or singles and were fitted with their own private bathrooms, were located on Main Deck. In general, there were five main decorative schemes used for these cabins. However, there were four special suites, two on each side of the ship, that were individually treated. The description, from a booklet issued by Cunard at the time of *Saxonia*'s entry into service, makes these suites sound as exotic as Cleopatra's barge. "M42 (bedroom) has a mauve and green carpet with a rope design; the walls are treated with beige lace on eau de nil Zapide and the dado rail is Maidu burr, used also for the beds with a banding of sapeli. The furniture is mahogany with cherry upholstery and the curtains are wine satin.... M44 – here the walls are in shadow wood and the dado, doors and also the beds are in walnut burr with eucalyptus banding.... The curtains are silver satin and the walnut furniture is upholstered in grey and white. Chequered rectangles of walnut burr and figured walnut have been used for the entrance passage.... M43 (bedroom) has the Dunmail rope design in red, white and blue in the carpet and the walls are finished dark grey with a black knot pattern. Grey sycamore has been used for the dado and doors, with cross grain grey sycamore for the beds; the furniture is mahogany upholstered in blue with a spotted design of red and white.... In the sitting room, the lighter-toned woods have been employed – the dado and doors in white burr, used also for the table tops.... The entrance passage uses chequered rectangles of white ash burr and brown oak burr. Green upholstery with the Dunmail rope design also in green and curtains of the knot design in green flecked with gold sustain the lightness of the theme." The remaining First Class accommodation, while furnished in less exotic materials, was nonetheless attractive in its varied colour schemes and its use of walnut, sycamore and mahogany panelling.

The Tourist Class passenger cabins were arranged on the Main, A, Restaurant and B decks and on Main deck there were blocks of cabins that were interchangeable between Tourist and First Class. These cabins, of course, had private bathrooms but the majority of the Tourist Class passengers had to make use of shared facilities. For a brand new ship, even in 1954, on what was one of the most prestigious of liner routes, this showed a remarkable lack of forward thinking on the part of the Cunard directors. To have built a liner on which, out of approximately 330 cabins, less than a third had the convenience of private bathrooms, seems rather short-

Cunard moves into the 1950s: *Saxonia*'s Drawing Room and Library *Author's collection.*

The Odahmin Restaurant. *Author's collection.*

sighted. The Tourist Class cabins were based around four different colour schemes of green, red, blue and brown.

A shared facility between the classes was the cinema. This was quite an ambitious room, when one considers the relatively modest tonnage of the ship. The auditorium extended through three decks and was divided into stalls and balcony. (The stalls were for the use of Tourist Class passengers, while First Class were up in the balcony.) There was seating for almost 300 and while the colour scheme was primarily red, the curtains framing the proscenium were "a hilariously gay Harlequin design in bright gold and black".

Saxonia's deck spaces were considered to be exceptional. For First Class passengers there was a large games area forward of the funnel on the Sports Deck, also an open promenade on Promenade Deck forward of the superstructure. The First Class glass-enclosed promenade followed the curve of the forward superstructure and extended aft to where the Tourist Class promenade began. Flanking the main public rooms for this class, the Tourist promenade led out onto a large games deck. Immediately below, on Main deck, there was further games space for the Tourist Class passengers. In addition, they had the use of a broad stretch of open space at the after end of the Sports Deck. A novel feature was that on these various open decks, the markings for the different games, normally painted lines, were inset into the deck in metal.

On the 2nd September, 1954, *Saxonia* departed Liverpool on her maiden voyage to Quebec and Montreal. She was under the command of Captain Andrew McKellar and, very importantly, she had a full complement of passengers. She arrived in Quebec on the 7th and remained in Montreal from the 8th to the 15th, when she set sail for Liverpool. It was a stormy crossing with gale force winds but nevertheless she arrived back in the River Mersey nine hours ahead of schedule. Despite the gales, *Saxonia* had managed to reduce the existing record for the crossing to Liverpool from just over five days to 4 days 23 hours 24 minutes, an average speed of 20.74 knots. It seemed as though she would be set for a long and successful career on the Canada run.

She continued to maintain the service between Liverpool and the St. Lawrence until late November, by which time the ice could be expected to be making the river impassable. On the 26th, she left Liverpool with 716 passengers aboard, bound for Cobh and Halifax and what would be her maiden arrival at New York. She steamed into the Hudson on the 5th December, 36 hours late, to be greeted by the traditional welcome of fireboats, sending up plumes of water, and a flotilla of other small craft as well as city officials. Spectators lined the shore. The voyage had been an unpleasant one and *Saxonia* had encountered headwinds of gale and hurricane force.

Ivernia

The *Ivernia* was launched on Tuesday, the 14th December, 1954, just nine days after the *Saxonia* steamed into New York for the first time. Originally, it had been arranged that the ceremony should be performed by the wife of the Canadian Prime Minister but plans had to be altered and, instead, Mrs. D. C. Howe, wife of the country's Minister of Trade, sent the ship down the ways. As with the wintertime launching of her sister, the *Ivernia*'s christening was not blessed with good weather. As she took to the water, she was caught by a strong crosswind. Very quickly, she found herself dangerously close to the river bank with her stern within just a few feet of a storage quay. It took six tugs to guide her out of danger and toward the fitting out berth.

Tugs take control of *Ivernia* after her launching. *Captain Ron Warwick collection.*

***Ivernia* at speed on her trials, June, 1955.** *Peter Kohler collection.*

The fitting out of the *Ivernia*, like that of the *Saxonia*, took nearly six months. On the 13th June, 1955, she sailed from Glasgow on a series of trials that lasted until the 17th. It had been the original intention that she would begin her maiden voyage from Liverpool to Quebec and Montreal on the 30th. However, Cunard were being hit by industrial disputes which brought about changes to these plans. The initial trouble had involved the catering staff of the *Ascania*, who went on strike. The action had quickly spread to other Cunard ships that happened to be in the Mersey at that time. *Saxonia* had been due to sail on the 13th but she was 90 crewmembers short. Her 730 passengers, waiting to embark, had to be sent home and *Saxonia* remained in the Mersey for two weeks before she was able to sail. On the 25th, Cunard announced that *Ivernia* would begin her maiden voyage from Greenock instead of Liverpool and she sailed from there, bound for Canada with 900 passengers, on the 1st July.

In external appearance, *Saxonia* and *Ivernia* were virtually identical. Internally, the layout was also very similar, though *Ivernia* carried 15 fewer passengers in First Class. Her principal public rooms in First Class were the Smoking Room, Library, Lounge and Cocktail Bar; while in Tourist Class there were the Smoking Room, Garden Lounge, Drawing Room, Library and Main Lounge and, of course, both classes had their own restaurants.

Like *Saxonia*, the *Ivernia* was imbued with strong Canadian decorative themes contained within very modern settings. This led to striking and, in some cases, rather remarkable results, as in the First Class Cocktail Bar. This was known as the Mounties Bar and was inspired by the deeds of the Royal Canadian Mounted Police. The walls were covered in fabric in shades of beige, brown and green, the design of which incorporated various indigenous trees, different styles of boots, canoes, locomotives and helicopters. The room was accented with bright red to reflect the Mounties' uniforms and the overall design paid tribute to the expression "The Mountie always gets his man". There were decorative wall panels of old and new means to that end. While no other room on the ship exhibited quite such originality, the First Class Restaurant was striking in its hard-edged glamour. The walls were covered with alternating panels of silvered glass bricks and of a vivid red marbled design. The floor was in two shades of grey and yellow and the black-stained sycamore-framed chairs were upholstered in a combination of blue, yellow and green. If nothing else, this room showed that, at least decoratively, Cunard was willing to move into the late 20th century. This was a bold decision that did not find favour with the die-hard Cunard traditionalists, who considered both *Saxonia* and *Ivernia* too modern, too flashy and not at all in the company style.

Ivernia arrived in Montreal, at the end of the first leg of her maiden voyage, on the 7th July and was back in Liverpool on the 19th. The two superb new liners settled on the route and illustrated well Cunard's commitment to the Canadian service. As was usual on that route, once the St. Lawrence became impassable due to winter ice, the

Modernity with slight classical touches: *Ivernia*'s Tourist Class Amber Lounge. *Laurence Dunn collection.*

Trendily herbaceous: *Ivernia*'s Garden Lounge gave a modern twist to the old-style winter garden.
Author's collection.

ships were transferred temporarily to the Liverpool – Halifax – New York run. *Ivernia*'s first such sailing left Liverpool on the 2nd December, 1955. She called at Cobh on the 3rd, Halifax on the 8th and made her maiden arrival into New York on the 10th. She remained there, unloading and loading her cargo until the 15th, when she set sail back to Liverpool, arriving just two days before Christmas. Her sailings to the St. Lawrence ports resumed in mid-April, 1956 and continued relatively uneventfully until the 18th November when she was damaged by a severe Atlantic storm while on an outward voyage. The damage was temporarily repaired while she was in Montreal. Then, instead of returning to Liverpool as usual, *Ivernia* sailed for London and arrived there on the 2nd December. It was her first visit to that port. She then made four further Atlantic sailings from London.

Carinthia

The order for the third ship, to be named *Carinthia*, had been confirmed with John Brown & Co. in October, 1953. In June, 1955, with construction well underway, Cunard announced that the launching would be a particularly special occasion. Her Royal Highness Princess Margaret had agreed to perform the naming ceremony. This made *Carinthia* only the fourth Cunarder to be launched by Royalty. The date was set for the 14th December. As it approached, there was an increased effort to ensure that the ship would be ready to receive her royal sponsor.

The west coast was being hit by particularly bad weather and heavy, driving rainstorms made it difficult for work to continue on the outside of the vessel. Much of it had to be done round the clock and under floodlights to ensure its completion. Then there was a further complication: 1,000 of John Brown's engineers made moves which threatened to delay the *Carinthia*. They decided to ban all piecework and overtime. The men claimed that the management's assurances that more money would be earned on piecework had come to

Cheers as Princess Margaret launches *Carinthia* on the 14th December, 1955.
Captain Ron Warwick collection.

Back to tradition: *Carinthia*'s Smoking Room. *Author's collection.*

nothing. The engineering shop steward said that the engineers were the lowest paid skilled labour in the yard (at that time they were earning 4s. 5d. per hour while manual workers were receiving 4s. 8d. per hour). Strike action seemed very likely. However, it all appears to have been resolved as *Carinthia* was ready to receive the Princess on what turned out to be another rainswept day.

Despite the weather, the Princess insisted on walking along the hull of the ship to examine the launching mechanism. In her speech, she described the occasion as happy and brilliant. There were 20,000 spectators, many of them provided with a grandstand view from the keel of the sister ship *Sylvania*, which was taking shape in the berth alongside. At the time of the launch, it was rumoured that the Princess would make a visit to Canada and would sail there aboard *Carinthia* on her maiden voyage. Sadly, this remained a rumour and the liner never received this additional royal patronage.

As an aside, it is interesting to note that on the following day, the 15th December (and also at a Glasgow shipyard, Fairfield's), the *Oxfordshire* was launched for the Bibby Line. Two totally different ships built for completely differing services, the *Carinthia* and the *Oxfordshire* would one day come together under the same ownership. Who could have imagined then, in mid-December 1955, that 42 years later the new Cunarder would replace a much-restyled *Oxfordshire* in cruise service out of Australia?

In her external appearance, *Carinthia* was almost identical to her two earlier sisters, with her curved stem, cruiser stern and large, dome-topped funnel. She had an overall length of 608 ft. 3ins. and was 80 ft. wide, with a gross tonnage of 21,946. She was constructed with a cellular double bottom giving a continuous watertight inner skin from peak to peak, with 20 watertight compartments between the inner and outer bottoms. Ten transverse bulkheads formed the main watertight divisions above the double bottom. The main propelling machinery and the boilers were constructed by John Brown & Co. and incorporated the latest improvements in steam turbines and water tube boilers. The machinery consisted of a twin-screw installation of geared turbines designed for steam at 550lbs per square inch gauge pressure and at 850 degrees Fahrenheit. Two interesting features of the engine room were the unusually high floor level, caused by arranging the piping beneath the floor in banks with passages between to allow easy access and inspection; and the metering of the steam to all engine room and ship's services.

Carinthia was fitted to carry 154 First Class and 714 Tourist Class passengers with some of the First Class cabins being interchangeable for Tourist Class use if demand required. Features of the First Class accommodation were the two fully air-conditioned three-roomed suites and the large number of single cabins.

In response to some of the harsh criticisms regarding the overtly modern interior styling of *Saxonia* and *Ivernia*, Cunard decided to adopt a more traditional approach for the décor of *Carinthia*. They chose a style which was much more in keeping with what a large proportion of their passengers had indicated they wanted and, indeed, expected. It was very North Atlantic and, of course, would ultimately limit any attempt at versatility to suit *Carinthia* to a cruising career. Not everyone greeted this news with pleasure. Shortly after she was launched and Cunard had announced their planned decorative approach to this latest addition to their fleet, the *Architect & Building News* of the 5th January, 1956 wrote "… A new Cunarder: the *Carinthia*, the third of four sister ships for the Cunard Line is, regardless of cost, to be decorated internally to re-create the past in terms of the present by using modern methods of construction to interpret some of the gems of historical interior design and decoration! Why? The Cunard Line has a wonderful record for seamanship, service and naval architecture but an abysmal one for interior decoration. Why do the directors still doll up their ships like bad stage sets?"

While the design world may have thrown up its collective hands in horror at Cunard's decision to return to a more traditional interior style, the less imaginative shipping press applauded the move. The *Shipping World*, in its feature on the new ship, wrote "... In her internal décor *Carinthia* is in complete contrast to the *Saxonia* and *Ivernia*. In the two earlier ships, the style was generally modern, with bold masses of colour and decoration wherever possible. The result was something which might perhaps be expected to appeal to the most uninhibited Canadian. In the *Carinthia* a return has been made to the past and in general it has been done very well. There is, of course, good justification for conjuring up the past in a passenger liner and particularly one with the notable traditions of a Cunard ship. The company has advertised "gracious living" as a sales point and a very good one, too, and this is inevitably associated in most people's minds with the spaciousness of the past and not with the conditions of today." However, the journal was not full of unquestioning praise and it went on to say "... a point of criticism to be made concerns the ceiling treatments which tend to be out of keeping with the rest of the spaces. Throughout the public rooms, particularly the furniture, walls and flooring materials are dignified but the deckheads have little or nothing of this... With crude hexagonal shapes or with bold lines on the skew instead of on the square, they detract from the well co-ordinated effect of the rest of the rooms."

In *Carinthia* the layout of the public rooms differed from that in her sisters in that all her principal First Class public rooms, except the Restaurant, were on the Promenade Deck. The Lounge spanned the superstructure almost amidships and was flanked on either side by the First Class Promenade. In the earlier ships, this was the position of the Tourist Smoking Room, which in *Carinthia* was at the after end of the Boat Deck, giving on to one of the three big areas of deck space for games and recreation available to Tourist Class passengers. The First Class Smoking Room, incorporating a cocktail bar, was forward on the Promenade Deck (following the curve of the bridge front) instead of on the Boat Deck as in the other two ships. An innovation, introduced as a new Tourist public room, was a soda fountain adjoining the Main Lounge. It contained every modern device for the preparation of sundaes, milk shakes and other soft drinks. The two barmen who served there were specially trained in the United States to create these confections correctly.

The First Class Smoking Room had linen fold panelled walls, a Tudor-style fireplace, Renaissance pendant plaster ceiling, X-frame chairs covered in a flame stitch pattern of red, grey, blue and beige and a handsome Turkish carpet laid over a tiled floor that resembled flagstones. This remarkable room gave a forward view through mullioned windows. These could be closed off by brass-studded, velvet-covered shutters instead of by curtains. The intended result was to recall the stout comfort of Tudor England. What the inhabitants of Tudor England would have made of the cocktail bar decorated in this same theme on the starboard side of the room is anyone's guess. The whole effect was nothing less than bizarre.

The Main Lounge was handsomely proportioned and contained bow windows on both port and starboard sides. There was an oval dance floor and the room was decorated in a strong green and pink, in Regency style. Among the decorative features of the room was an 18th century clock veneered in tortoiseshell and set on a silvered stand. The Sports Deck Lounge was the only public room in First Class that escaped the heavy hand of period styling. Instead, this bright and airy room appears to have had a fresh modern, ocean liner style about its décor and was designed for a variety of purposes such as tea dances and cocktail parties as well as indoor sports such as table tennis.

The First Class Restaurant recalled the French rococo style with its walls panelled in grey sycamore veneer. Engraved mirrors with golden margins adorned the walls and a mural by Margot Gilbert, "Dinner At Versailles", gave an indication of the period chosen for the style of the room. A further link with the past was that the room was furnished with chairs that had once graced the Dining Room of the *Aquitania*. (Each of these chairs carried a small brass plate engraved to that effect.) Elsewhere in the ship, there were other items of furniture and carpets from both *Aquitania* and *Samaria*.

Tourist Class public rooms did not escape the "period" touches either. The Smoking Room and Cocktail Bar were situated on Boat Deck and were similar in theme to their First Class counterparts. The walls were covered in oak panelling consisting of small, alternately raised and sunken sections and meant to evoke an Elizabethan feel. Around the room was a continuous plaster frieze, but instead of Elizabethan ornament, it depicted the life of the Canadian beaver. The windows were mullioned and could be covered by shutters decorated with metal grillwork over flame-coloured leather cloth.

The largest public room on the ship was the Tourist Class Lounge. This was on the Promenade Deck and was treated in a style reminiscent of Renaissance interiors. There were large bow windows on both sides of the room and there was an orchestra platform and dance floor. The Soda Fountain had large doors leading out to the starboard side of the Promenade Deck. Its décor was described as "a fantasy based on the light iron trellis of Victorian verandas...; gaiety is the keynote and is achieved partly by the light fittings in the form of Chinese lanterns". Extending the full width of the ship, the Tourist Class Restaurant seated almost 500 passengers and like the other principal public rooms, was fully air-conditioned. It was decorated with broad panels and groups of slender

The First Class Restaurant, furnished with dining chairs from *Aquitania*. *Author's collection.*

pilasters typical of Pompeian decoration. These were faced with plastic in black, terracotta and green and topped by a frieze of Pompeian subjects painted in terracotta and gold on a background of black. As in the earlier ships, there was a cinema that served both classes and for its decorative style it used an old-fashioned theatre as its model. Both classes had several other smaller rooms, such as drawing rooms and libraries.

Several articles appeared in a variety of design journals regarding the interior décor and, again, not all of them were in favour of the "historical" themes used. However, most of them applauded the imaginative use of modern materials such as plastic, Terylene, vynide and perspex to create the varying decorative effects. According to Cunard, the reaction of the travelling public to the décor and furnishings of *Carinthia* was of almost unanimous approval.

Apart from the extensive passenger accommodations, the *Carinthia*, like her sisters, was built with considerable cargo space. Her five holds had a capacity of 290,000 cubic ft. for general cargo and 15,000 cubic ft. for insulated produce. Six hatches were fitted, of which No. 1 had a hinged steel cover on the weather deck while the remainder were fitted with MacGregor covers. The three aft were of the flush hatch type. For working cargo, eight steel derrick posts, four forward and four aft, were arranged to carry 14 derricks, 12 of which had a working load of 5 tons each and two were for up to 10 tons each.

Having been fitted out, *Carinthia* was dry-docked at Elderslie in preparation for her speed trials off the Isle of Arran. She departed John Brown's on the 12th June, 1956 and should have been ready to run the measured mile on the 13th. However, it was discovered that her bearings were running hot and her trials were delayed for several hours. The ship stood off the Tail of Bank while the trouble was corrected. The fault turned out to be a minor one and at 8.15 pm she set sail down the Firth. While on her speed trials, she passed and exchanged greetings with the inbound *Ivernia*. In May, it had been announced that Captain McKellar would be transferred from *Saxonia* to take command of *Carinthia*. At a luncheon held aboard the newly completed ship, Mr. F.H. Dawson, the General Manager of Cunard, announced that the *Saxonia* and *Ivernia* would be repositioned to Southampton. The object of the move was that, with a call at Le Havre, the line would be able to capture some of the traffic between the Continent and Canada. *Carinthia* and her yet to be completed sister *Sylvania* would still be based in Liverpool.

With everything satisfactory, *Carinthia* was officially handed over to Cunard Line and she set sail for Liverpool, arriving there on the 17th June. On the 27th, she embarked over 800 passengers for her maiden voyage to Canada. It had been hoped that she would make the crossing in record time but she was delayed for five hours by fog off Newfoundland. Her crossing to Quebec had taken 4 days 21 hours 6 minutes at an average speed of 20.91 knots. On her return voyage to Liverpool, she carried 890 passengers. Captain McKellar said of his ship, "She handles very well and we had a good, quiet and uneventful round voyage."

Although it was planned that the four new ships would replace the old, pre-War vessels that were also running in the Canadian service, at the time that *Carinthia* arrived on the scene the *Franconia, Ascania* and *Scythia* were fully employed. There was speculation for a time that there was sufficient demand for more than just the four new liners and that perhaps further tonnage would be ordered once the *Sylvania* had been delivered. It proved, however, to be little more than speculation. On the 12th October, 1956, it was announced that both *Franconia* and *Ascania* would be withdrawn from service the following month. Early in 1957, *Scythia* was transferred to the Liverpool – New York run and in January, 1958 she was sold for scrap. The Canada service was thus in the hands of the new quartet of liners. While perhaps eclipsed by the glamour of the *Queen Elizabeth, Queen Mary* and *Caronia*, the new Canadian ships were undoubtedly stars in their own right in the Cunard fleet.

At the time of her entry into service, it had been announced that *Carinthia* would undertake a "dollar-earning cruise" out of New York to the Caribbean during the forthcoming Christmas and New Year. She had maintained her St. Lawrence sailings up until December. Then in mid-December she departed Liverpool, via Cobh and Halifax, for New York. It turned out to be for many aboard a most memorable crossing. She made her first-ever arrival in Halifax on the 20th, about 50 hours behind schedule and several of her officers described the voyage as the worst Atlantic crossing in their memories. A succession of storms had pounded the liner almost continually from the day that she departed Cobh until she was just a few miles off Chebucto Head and approaching Halifax. While some of her passengers were bruised as they were tossed about by the heaving seas, no one suffered any broken bones and the ship came through the heavy weather without any damage - a remarkable fact when one looks at an abstract of her log for the voyage:

Dec. 13 (after leaving Cobh) – strong westerly gales, very high sea.
Dec. 14 southwest to west storm, precipitous seas, very heavy swell.
Dec. 15 precipitous seas.
Dec. 16 whole west to northwest gale, very high seas.
Dec. 17 strong northwest gale.
Dec. 18 strong northwest gale backing to moderate.
Dec. 19 fresh southwest breeze veering to strong northwest gales.

The passage from Liverpool to Halifax had taken 7 days 14 hours and 12 minutes during which the ship had averaged 12.35 knots though at times she was forced to slow to just 6 knots. Two days later, she left New York on the first cruise to be operated by one of the *Saxonia* sisters and, after such a rough crossing, her crew must have found considerable pleasure in the placid warmth of the Caribbean. The fourteen-day cruise took her to Martinique, Trinidad, La Guaira, Curaçao, Cristobal and Port au Prince, arriving back in New York on the 6th January, 1957.

Sylvania

In March, 1955, Cunard Line gave John Brown the confirmation of their order for the final ship in the quartet, *Sylvania*. The first section of her keel was laid on the 9th November, 1955 in the adjacent berth to *Carinthia*, which was just a month away from her launching. At the time, there were doubts whether the *Carinthia* would be ready for the launch, owing to serious industrial troubles at the shipyard. Later, there were similar doubts over the launching of the *Sylvania*, which was scheduled for the 22nd November, 1956. Luckily, however, the work was a month ahead of schedule and in the end the industrial troubles did not delay the launching. Mrs. Norman A. Robertson, wife of the Canadian High Commissioner in London, performed the ceremony. *Sylvania* proved to be the unique ship among the sisters in that she had the good fortune to be launched in fine weather. In a speech given after the launch ceremony, Mrs. Robertson said that she hoped "… it would not be long before Britons could visit Canada with the same ease that Canadians can visit Britain". This ease of travel was soon to be available, but who could see at that time just how rapidly the mode of travel was about to change?

In 1954, when *Saxonia* entered service, the future still looked rosy for trans-Atlantic liners. The World was beginning to return to something like normal after the ravages of war, people were looking to start new lives in distant countries and tourism was on an upward swing as never before. The planned new Canadian quartet seemed

***Sylvania* nears completion in the fitting-out basin.** *Laurence Dunn collection.*

ideal to meet these challenges with their emphasis on Tourist Class accommodations. That year, according to the Trans-Atlantic Passenger Conference, over 900,000 passengers were carried across the North Atlantic and this included the Canadian trade. The numbers increased steadily, reaching a peak in 1958 when over 1,036,000 passengers sailed across the Atlantic. The Conference announced in New York in July, 1958, that nearly 10 per cent more people had gone by ship from New York to Europe during the first half of the year than in the same period of 1957. This accounted for 230,000 passengers – a new record for a six-month period. However, just as the figures reached these dizzy heights, the first commercial jet aircraft was introduced between Europe and New York and there was an instantaneous effect on the number of people who chose to cross by sea. After an immediate decline, for a year or two the number of passengers remained steady at about 800,000. But the decline was there and for ships like the *Saxonia* and her sisters, built without any real thought toward even occasional use as cruise ships, this was bad news indeed.

Sadly, *Sylvania* arrived on the scene just too late. For only a little over a year she was able to bask in the glory that was trans-Atlantic liner service at its absolute peak. The speech given by the General Manager of Cunard Line aboard *Sylvania* on the eve of her maiden voyage was full of optimism but it was based on the previous passenger figures of her sister ships. The line, like many others, had not fully considered the threat the jet aircraft was about to pose to their future or the need to give their new ships greater versatility. They had continued to design and build liners in the same style as those originating in the days before the jet engine was even thought of. As built, *Saxonia, Ivernia, Carinthia* and *Sylvania* were totally unsuited to use as cruise ships. They were purely trans-Atlantic liners.

In that final glow of optimism, *Sylvania* sailed from Glasgow on the 3rd June, 1957 on her trials off the Scottish coast. Her maiden voyage began from Greenock for Quebec and Montreal on the 5th. The round trip ended in Liverpool on the 20th.

Sylvania had the same profile as her three sisters and her internal arrangement followed the same pattern as that of *Carinthia*. The four ships, while all but identical on the outside, were in fact two pairs and remained so for their entire lives. Like the others, *Sylvania* was able to carry considerable quantities of freight: 290,000 cubic ft. of general cargo and 12,000 cubic ft. of insulated cargo. Again, Cunard chose to look back to period styles to decorate the public spaces of the ship. This time, the treatment was influenced by the seventeenth and eighteenth centuries and the brief for the designers was to recreate some of the gems of that time, again using modern materials. Many of the designers who had worked on the interiors of the previous three ships worked on *Sylvania*. Denise Bates, Arthur Fleischmann, Foster Fletcher, Margot Gilbert, Tom Luzny, Peter Stanton and Rana Stryck were among the artists who contributed murals and decorative features.

The First Class Sports Deck Lounge was located forward on that deck and the emphasis in this spacious room was observation. A raised platform gave uninterrupted views to port and starboard over the lifeboats. An attractively furnished cocktail bar was a feature and a large wall map of the Atlantic enabled passengers to follow the route with the aid of model ships – an idea borrowed from the *Queen Mary*. The floor of the room was inlaid with a large-scale chessboard and draughts board and there was also provision for table tennis and other games.

Located forward on the Promenade Deck was the First Class Smoking Room and Cocktail Bar. Here, the decorative theme was based on badges of the British Army and its Canadian counterparts. The heraldic nature and the composition and colour of the badges formed a resplendent frieze with further badges massed both above the bar and over the fireplace. The navy blue and red dress uniform cloth, embroidered with crowns, stars and gold lace chevrons, which faced the shutters to the mullioned windows, completed the distinctive army atmosphere of the room. The First Class Lounge was modelled on the boudoir of Madame de Serilly. It was panelled in grey sycamore which was embellished with gold aluminium mouldings and decorated mirrors. The ivory lacquered furniture was covered with delicate damask woven in what looked like silk but was, in fact, Terylene. This room had an oval dance floor and bay windows both to port and starboard.

The Library was forward of the Lounge, the bookcases, woodwork and furniture being of mahogany while the walls were treated in green hide. Attractive gold-coloured upholstery contrasted effectively with the shades of green in the walls and carpet. The glass fronts of the bookcases were shaped in a series of bays and a special arrangement of fittings at the top of the bookcases reflected the light onto the spines of the books. Aft of the Lounge was the First Class Drawing Room. It was furnished in a sedate Regency style in sage green and wine and this room was reserved for non-smokers – quite forward-thinking for 1957. Finely figured walnut contrasted with intricate markings of white ash burr in First Class Restaurant. The decoration surrounding the rectangular mirror features was executed in the style of old Sheffield plate. The chairs were an adaptation of a very early eighteenth-century style in walnut. Again, Terylene was used in the upholstery, the pattern being that of a traditional floral spray.

The First Class cabins were all on the Main Deck and each had an adjoining bath or shower. While the designers had been called upon to make extensive use of modern materials in their creation of *Sylvania*'s interiors, a wide range of traditional yet exotic wood veneers was nevertheless used in the finish of the First Class accommodations. These included abenita, pear, apple and white ash burr, while the furniture was made of walnut or mahogany with veneers of amboyna, Rhodesian walnut, marble makore, rose zebrano and draped kevazingo. On

***Sylvania* continued the return to traditional décor: the Tourist Class Lounge and Bar.**
Author's collection and Laurence Dunn collection.

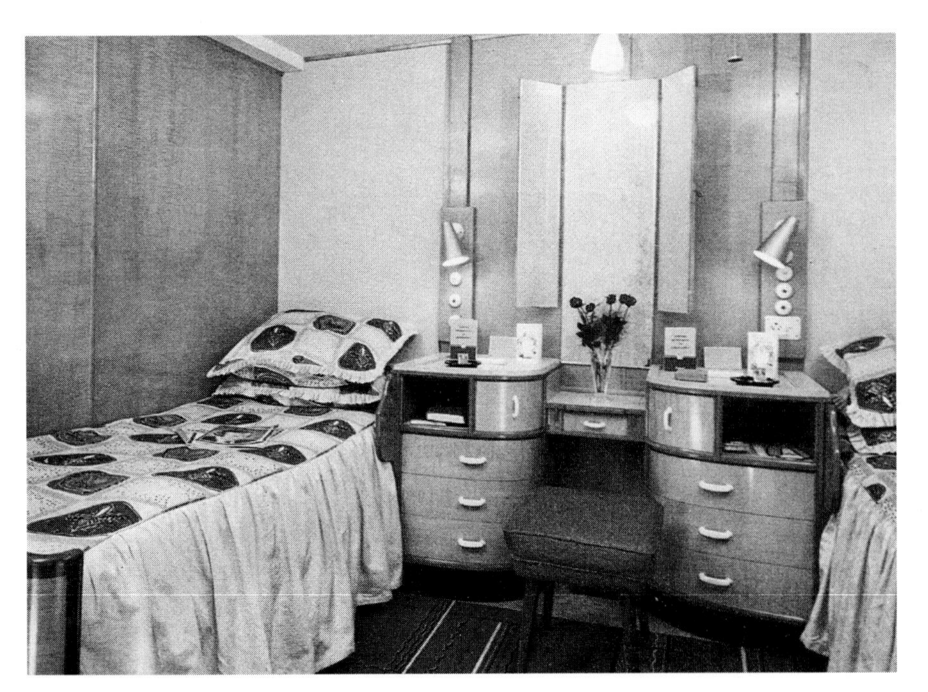

A stylish First Class stateroom. *Captain Ron Warwick collection.*

each side of the Main Deck there was a three-roomed suite, comprising a bedroom, sitting room and dining room.

As on the sister ships, there was a 300-seat cinema that extended through three decks. A rare Canadian marble was specially obtained in order to reproduce the columns of scagiola, which were the outstanding feature of the Tourist Class Lounge. The Tourist Class Smoking Room, at the after end of the Boat Deck, featured seventeen murals, each one depicting proverbs from different European countries. Below each painting was the proverb in the original language as well as a translation. Between the murals, the walls were panelled in both oak and ash. Large mullioned windows gave views to port, starboard and over the Sports Deck. The main decorative theme of the Tourist Class Restaurant was the harvesting of fruit and this was depicted in various murals around the room. The main colour scheme was white and gold and the room was furnished with satinwood chairs upholstered in three pastel shades, green, pink and blue. The other public rooms for Tourist Class were a library and a drawing room.

The Tourist Class cabins were located on Main, A, Restaurant and B Decks and were arranged for either two or four passengers. None of the Tourist Class cabins, with the exception of two blocks that were interchangeable between First and Tourist, had private bathrooms. For Tourist Class, even on Cunard's newest liner in 1957, a trip to the bathroom meant shared facilities down the hall.

With *Sylvania* in service, the four new ships maintained their regular services to Canada and Cunard was justifiably proud in advertising six sailings each month on the route, with *Sylvania* occasionally calling at Greenock. After barely five months in service, in early November, *Sylvania* encountered a severe storm while en route to Canada and suffered some damage as a result. On the 17th December, she made her first arrival in New York and on the 21st she departed on a Christmas and New Year cruise to Port au Prince, Curaçao, Cristobal, Havana – where she spent New Year's Eve – and Nassau. However, as with *Carinthia*'s similar cruise the previous year, it was purely a token gesture towards cruising for on the 10th January, 1958 *Sylvania* resumed her trans-Atlantic service and on the 5th April returned to the Canadian run.

The dining room of a First Class Suite. *Laurence Dunn collection.*

Sisters Together

Saxonia and *Ivernia*

On the 7th June, 1957, while *Sylvania* was just two days into her maiden voyage and the quartet of liners was now complete, *Saxonia* departed Montreal for Le Havre and Southampton to begin the previously announced service between Canada and the Hampshire port. She made her first arrival there on the 14th June and began the regular service just five days later. *Ivernia* had already made her appearance in Southampton on the 23rd March at the end of a crossing from New York. On the 1st April, she had sailed on a short cruise that had taken her to Cherbourg, Plymouth, back to Cherbourg and then returned to Southampton on the 5th.

While Saxonia aimed to capture some of the continental traffic by making a call at Le Havre, *Ivernia*'s sailings often included Rotterdam. She made her first call at the Dutch port on the 7th October and sailed directly from there to Quebec. She made several more sailings of this kind until early December when she returned to Southampton. On the 24th January, 1958, *Saxonia* arrived in the Port of London for the first time and her winter sailings to New York were all made from the Thames until the 25th April, when she resumed the service to Canada. It was not until mid-June that she returned to

Saxonia, handling cargo in a wintry New York with Greek Line's _Arkadia_ in the opposite berth.
Peter Kohler collection.

Southampton. In October, 1960 and again in November, 1961 *Saxonia* had her voyages extended to include calls at Rotterdam. In January, 1962, *Saxonia* was again in Liverpool and she sailed from there to New York. In March, there was a further diversion from her regular route when she sailed from New York to St. John, New Brunswick and Bremerhaven. Having arrived there on the 14th, she sailed the following day for St. John, N.B. and New York, making a return to Southampton via Halifax, Cobh and Le Havre.

Coincidentally, April of 1960, 1961 and 1962 all proved to be unlucky months for Ivernia. On the 8th April, 1960, she struck the passenger gangway as she was coming alongside the Tilbury Landing Stage. On the 13th April, 1961, although the Canadian service had resumed, there was still a great deal of ice around and while in the Gulf of St. Lawrence she suffered ice damage. On her return to Southampton on the 25th, she ran aground off Hythe but luckily an inspection revealed her to be undamaged. Unfortunately, this was not to be the case in April, 1962. This time her propellers were sufficiently damaged by ice while she was navigating her way along the St. Lawrence for her to need dry-docking for repairs before she could make the return voyage.

In June, 1962, there was a meeting of shareholders of Cunard, presided over by Sir John Brocklebank, the Chairman of the company. He was faced with the unpleasant task of explaining losses for the line of £1,700,000 during the previous financial year. Sir John tried to give the shareholders his assurances that the directors were seeking the best possible advice regarding the future of the fleet. He announced that both *Saxonia* and *Ivernia* would be taken out of service and given an extensive rebuild and restyling that would make them more suited for cruising. Both ships continued with their Atlantic service for a few more months but on the 5th September *Saxonia* departed Southampton for her final voyage under that name, returning on the 21st. She had completed 116 round voyages across the Atlantic. On the 25th, she sailed for the Clyde, back to her birthplace and the hands of John Brown's, who had been entrusted with the task of giving her and her sister the transformation that would allow them a fresh start. *Ivernia*'s final Atlantic round voyage, her 109th, had begun on the 19th September and she was back in Southampton on the 5th October. On the 11th, she too arrived at John Brown's.

Carinthia and *Sylvania*

Soon after that first Christmas and New Year cruise in 1956-7, *Carinthia* was back in Liverpool undergoing a brief overhaul. However, the work had to be left incomplete as she was recalled to service. Because of the Suez crisis, the annual Mediterranean cruise of the last remaining White Star liner, *Britannic,* had been cancelled and as a result the schedule of sailings from Liverpool had been upset. In February, *Carinthia* was in the news again when it was reported that two fires had broken out in Tourist Class cabins, one during a recent voyage to New York and the other after the ship had berthed there. Both fires were attributed to careless passengers leaving cigarettes smouldering and were said to have been unrelated. And, before the ship had departed Liverpool, it had been discovered that several of the mailbags she was due to carry had been tampered with, but the police were unable to establish whether any items were missing. Perhaps it was just a voyage of coincidences, but maybe not.......

On the 16th October, 1957, at Liverpool, *Carinthia* suffered slight shell door damage while leaving Sandon Dock for the Princes Landing Stage to embark passengers. In April, 1959, she had one of her propellers damaged by ice in Montreal harbour. She was not inspected until her arrival back at Liverpool, when it was discovered that her starboard propeller had been so badly buckled that it was necessary to replace it. As a result of this unscheduled dry-docking, she left Liverpool 24 hours late and in order to help catch up with her schedule the usual call at Greenock was omitted. Passengers who had planned to board her there had instead to be transported down to Liverpool. Later that year, *Carinthia* made some deviations from her normal Liverpool route. She made her first call at Rotterdam on the 31st October and remained there until the 2nd November. Then on the 20th November, she made her debut at Southampton. In April, 1960, she made a record-breaking crossing between Montreal and Greenock. The voyage took 5 days 6 hours and 27 minutes, the liner averaging 21.8 knots. The perfect conditions were an obvious help and her Master, Captain Geoffrey Marr described them as "summer cruise weather".

In November, 1960, the Canadian government chartered *Carinthia* for some trooping voyages. This short charter came to an end on the 15th December, when the last brigade of Canadian troops were disembarked at Halifax. She then sailed for New York to embark passengers for Liverpool. What should have been a regular trans-Atlantic crossing turned out to be one that caused nothing but bad publicity for the line. *Carinthia* sailed from New York on the 23rd December. On Christmas Night, several crewmembers discovered, after coming off duty, that the Chief Officer had closed their bar 45 minutes earlier than usual. About fifty crewmembers, both stewards and deckhands, decided to protest and went to the Tourist Class Lounge where a dance was being held. They mingled with the passengers and demanded to see the Master, Captain Marr. Officers tried to persuade the men to leave but, when they would not go, the passengers were asked to join the Purser for cocktails in the Smoking Room while Captain Marr tried to deal with the incident. Having heard their complaints, he ordered their bar re-opened for an hour. However, the following morning, 32 of the protesters were disciplined and fined one day's pay. The incident was widely reported in the press.

Carinthia had been the centre of a dispute the previous July when four crewmembers, who had been playing electric guitars in the crew quarters in the early hours of the morning, had been disciplined after complaints from passengers who had been unable to sleep. The crewmembers had refused an order to stop playing and as a result had been fined one day's pay. This sparked off a 10-week strike, which spread to most of the ports in Britain and became a wages and hours issue. The publicity from these incidents did nothing but tarnish the image of Cunard.

On the 14th March, 1961, The *Greenock Telegraph* reported that "... *Carinthia*'s winter stay in dock for the usual seasonal overhaul has been considerably extended, but it is because of the Merseyside shiprepairers' strike. The liner was in dock at Liverpool when the dispute began at the start of the year and as a result of the hold up has already missed three sailings. The *Carinthia* was scheduled to operate on the Greenock – New York service with the *Sylvania* and should have been at the Tail of the Bank on the 28th January, 25th February and 17th March. Now it seems as if she will also have to forego a call on the 25th March." Passengers who had been booked to sail on that voyage were transferred to other Cunard liners sailing from Southampton and cargo scheduled to be carried on *Carinthia* travelled in a chartered vessel instead. Apart from *Carinthia*, several other ships were affected. The winter overhaul of the cargo/passenger liner *Parthia* was held up and she missed two round voyages. The annual overhaul of her sister ship *Media* had to be postponed and she maintained the line's North Atlantic service from Liverpool with *Sylvania*. The strike was over a change in the system of payment, which would have meant about £1 per week extra for the engineers; this resulted in nearly 3,000 other ship repair workers being laid off.

Liner traffic to and from Tail of the Bank for those first months of 1961 had all been to New York. The Clyde – Canada runs were scheduled to begin at the end of March with a sailing of the Canadian Pacific liner *Empress of Britain*. On the same day *Sylvania* was expected inbound from New York. Despite the continued increase of competition by the airlines, there were still sufficient numbers of passengers on the Canada run for two liners to be scheduled to be in Greenock anchorage together on several occasions during that summer. The port authorities expressed concern at the congestion in the Customs shed with so many passengers to be dealt with.

Carinthia narrowly avoided a real disaster on the 30th August, 1961. She was bound for Montreal from Liverpool and Greenock when, in thick fog 30 miles west of Quebec, she collided with the 7,013 ton Canadian ship *Tadoussac*. Both vessels were damaged, the *Tadoussac* having windows and lifeboats smashed, but luckily there were no casualties on either ship. *Carinthia* had 873 passengers aboard at the time. It was reported that only frantic last minute manoeuvres by the pilots of each ship had avoided a head on collision. Despite the incident, *Carinthia* arrived in Montreal only 30 minutes late and departed for Britain on schedule.

Carinthia's Atlantic crossings from the 19th April to late May, 1962 were all cancelled due to strike action and she was not able to resume her sailings until the 31st May. Then in July she had a most unusual departure from her normal trans-Atlantic route, leaving Montreal on the 20th for Gdansk in Poland. A somewhat more glamorous diversion occurred in 1963 when she made a call at Bermuda on the 25th January while en route to New York and a further call was made there in February. A strike by longshoremen in the St. Lawrence River that October caused considerable disruption to the Canadian service. *Carinthia*, carrying 203 passengers, was diverted to Halifax, arriving there on the 10th October. She continued to use Halifax as her turn-around port until the strike was resolved. Canadian Pacific's flagship, *Empress of Canada*, had been less successful. She had attempted to dock at the strikebound Quebec harbour the previous day but had been unable to do so and as a result was anchored in mid-river with her 409 passengers not knowing where or when they might be disembarked.

In January, 1964 one of *Carinthia*'s crossings to New York was made via Bermuda. However, even the added attraction of a call at this lovely island was insufficient to lure many passengers aboard for that mid-winter crossing and she was carrying only 260. In her holds there were just 1,800 tons of cargo. On the return voyage there was a marginally healthier passenger load, 480 in all, but her cargo holds were even emptier, with a mere 250 tons of freight. It could hardly have been worth the effort to load it. Considering the fact that the ship had the capacity for 868 passengers and 10,000 tons of freight, these figures must have been a sure indication to Cunard of just how inappropriate was the design of these liners.

Sylvania was destined to serve the Canada run for only a relatively short time. It was reported on the 30th November, 1960 that as from the following April she would replace the *Britannic* (which at the time of the announcement was on her final voyage) in the company's Liverpool – New York service. Actually, *Sylvania* had already begun her scheduled winter run to New York; her final voyage to Canada had taken place during the first weeks of November. On replacing *Britannic* on the New York run, she made regular calls at Cobh and occasional ones at Greenock and Halifax. She remained in this service through the summer and winter of 1961 and 1962. There were, however, occasional diversions: on the 22nd March, 1962 she left New York for Greenock and Liverpool but also called at Bermuda; and on the 6th April she made a call at Amsterdam on her way back to New York. During 1963, like her sister *Carinthia*, she made two further calls at Bermuda as part of her Atlantic crossings, one on the 23rd February and then in March a longer stay over the 23rd and 24th. In April, she had a sailing delayed due to engine problems but otherwise *Sylvania* appears to have led a relatively blameless career on the Atlantic run. There were further minor changes to her route at the end of May and in July, 1964 when she visited Boston.

The "New Look" Cunarders

Saxonia had arrived back at the Clydebank yard on the 27th September, 1962 to undergo the extensive refit that Chairman Sir John Brocklebank had announced at the June meeting of shareholders. The refit was to involve considerable structural alterations and out would go those very contemporary Canadian-themed interiors that had so disconcerted the traditionalists. Instead, she would be given a completely fresh décor before taking up her new role as a dual-purpose Atlantic liner and cruise ship. It had been announced earlier that month that not only would the *Saxonia* and *Ivernia* be remodelled, they would also be given new names. *Saxonia* would be rechristened *Carmania* and *Ivernia* would be called *Franconia* – names associated with previous famous cruising ships of the fleet. Cunard's plan was to operate both ships between Southampton and the St. Lawrence during the summer, with calls at Rotterdam, but during the winter months they were to switch to cruise service from Port Everglades to the West Indies.

Carmania was the first of the pair to emerge from the builders' yard; gone were the traditional black hull and white upperworks of an Atlantic liner. Now she was resplendent in Cunard's cruising livery of four shades of pale green. It was the 1st April, 1963 and 450 representatives of the travel trade and shipping press boarded the ship for a short shakedown cruise through the Irish Sea to Southampton. It was obvious to those aboard that the change of name symbolised a complete change of personality for the ship. The newly-found elegance of her décor was the result of co-operation between Cunard,

During *Saxonia*'s conversion into *Carmania*, she was given an extensive Lido. *Captain Ron Warwick collection.*

John Brown's and a very talented team of designers, Jean Munro, Evelyn Pinching, Michael Inchbald and Paul Gell. Paul Gell had very recently been responsible for the stunning interiors on the direct competitor to these restyled Cunarders, Canadian Pacific's *Empress of Canada*.

Apart from new décor, all the public rooms had been renamed. The forwardmost room on the Promenade Deck was now called the St. Lawrence Bar and its striking décor included a rich seaweed-coloured carpet, providing the background to gold curtains with chairs and sofas upholstered in a blue and brown floral pattern. Other chairs were covered either in a coral tweed fabric or in pale gold leather. The walls were covered in a cream textured plastic material and were hung with old prints. Cane work fronted the horseshoe-shaped bar on the port side of the room. Just aft on the port side was the Library, with predominantly green furnishings

A lounge on two levels: the Island Club and the Nantucket Room.
Captain Ron Warwick collection.

The First Class Lounge was now transformed into the Albany Room. Here the colour scheme comprised very pale grey walls with a two-tone grey carpet and chairs and sofas upholstered either in yellow or coral tweed or in grey silk. There was one sofa that was covered in yellow floral-patterned linen and this same fabric was used for the curtains. The circular dance floor remained and a yellow, tented structure hung over the orchestra stand. The central part of the opposite, forward wall had been covered in mirror, giving the illusion of great space; and the lighting came from two specially-designed black and gilt chandeliers and from wall sconces. Between the principal First and Tourist Class public rooms were the hairdressing salons, shop, Tourist Class Library and Drawing Room. The latter could be converted for use for religious services. Also at this point was the balcony to the cinema, its red and gold décor little changed.

Furthest aft of the public rooms was the Tourist Class Nantucket Room and it was to this space that the greatest internal changes had been made. It was already the largest public room on the ship, but now its transformation had given it splendid proportions. Slightly raised side wings, which extended the room to the full width of the ship, provided vantage points for watching the dancing or cabaret by night or a pleasant sea view by day. The room was carpeted in green and the chairs were covered in fabric of turquoise or blackberry or yellow and the curtains were of blue silk. There was a large dance floor with an orchestra platform at its forward end. The room had been lengthened aft and a graceful Y-shaped staircase led up to a large gallery known as the Island Club, perhaps the most attractive space aboard the newly refitted liner. This was on Boat Deck and had its own dance floor and bar. The walls were covered with deep green canvas and at the windows there were two sets of curtains, blue chintz for day and blackberry silk for night. Tables and seating placed around the balcony provided a perfect viewpoint for the dancing or cabaret and by day the room was a superb observation lounge with its large windows on both sides and looking aft. The chief feature of the room was a large mural by Felix Kelly, a painting of the snow-covered Main Street of Nantucket, famed for the perfection of its 18th century architecture.

Both the Island Club and the Nantucket Room opened onto the lido area. In order to provide for the lengthening of the Nantucket Room and the creation of the lido, three hatches and their associated cargo handling gear were entirely removed. The focal point of the lido deck was a pale blue tiled, kidney-shaped swimming pool, 33 ft. long and 16 ft. wide. Glass screens, rather larger than the adjacent Promenade Deck windows, had been built at the ship's sides to shelter the lido and gracefully curved staircases led from the Promenade Deck up to the Boat Deck. Infra-red heaters were installed to make the deck useable even during cool weather. On Main Deck, the Ten Pin Club had been created for teenagers. It had a two-lane ten pin bowling alley, table tennis tables, a machine dispensing soft drinks, a jukebox and a dance floor.

Both the dining rooms had also been totally restyled. That for the First Class was now known as The Garden Restaurant. It was carpeted in green and the chairs were either upholstered in a bright pink or in moss green. Although the room did not extend to the sides of the ship, the illusion of windows was created with concealed lighting shining down onto curtains of a floral pattern in shades of pink. The Tourist Class Dining Room was now

Given grander proportions by the clever use of mirrors, *Carmania*'s First Class Albany Room. *Author's collection.*

A fresh, new look: *Carmania*'s First Class Sun Room. *Author's collection.*

called the Tivoli Restaurant. The engine casing that went up through this room was now faced in mirrors which were framed with barley twist columns. The carpet was in blue/grey and the chairs were upholstered in either blue, pale yellow or red. The portholes were covered with louvred blinds and each pair was draped with blue floral chintz curtains.

Carmania's passenger capacity had been reduced, thus giving room for increased amenities. Full air-conditioning had been installed throughout both passenger and crew accommodation and practically all passenger cabins had been given their own bath or shower and toilet. The transformation of the Tourist Class cabins was of such a high standard that it was now difficult to tell them apart from those in First Class. Both classes had been fitted with clean-lined modern furniture, imaginative lighting and what was described as "simple but glowing colour schemes." Although there had been a reduction in the number of passengers carried, some new cabins had been created. For example, five splendid First Class cabins now occupied the forward-facing space that had previously been the First Class Smoking Room.

Throughout the ship, the accent was on strong, plain colours. Decorative items were limited but used to great effect. *Carmania*, in fact, showed that a British liner could be stylish. Black and white sofas with coral cushions placed in a foyer, an elegant Regency table in the Nantucket Room or a strategically placed antique mirror all helped to show that, while the Canadian-themed rooms may have been right when the ship entered service as *Saxonia* nine years earlier, now as *Carmania* she was ready to create an impression on the travelling public all over again. Even so, there were those, with more traditional

Sober comfort in First Class . *Author's collection.*

Deck games beneath the utterly distinctive funnel. *Captain Ron Warwick collection.*

The Tourist Class Mayflower Room and Cactus Club on *Franconia* contrast interestingly with the equivalent rooms on *Carmania*. *Author's collection.*

tastes, who felt that the "new look" was still very "un-Cunard".

Apart from the enhanced public rooms and cabins, much had been done behind the scenes to make *Carmania* a more effective cruise ship. Her fuel oil capacity was substantially increased and she was fitted with two evaporators capable of producing 350 tons daily of fresh water from seawater. Additional facilities for passengers were installed, such as three launderettes. Four specially designed glass fibre launches replaced the conventional lifeboats for transporting passengers from the ship to the shore when she was at anchor during cruises. The original air-conditioning plant was increased to cope with the fact that all the accommodation was now to have the benefit of this amenity.

Within a few weeks of her re-entry into service, the *Carmania* was joined by the refitted and re-styled *Ivernia*, now called *Franconia*. She too was painted in the cruising green livery. The re-styling of *Franconia* followed very closely that of *Carmania*, with the removal of the aft cargo-handling gear, hatches and holds making room for an almost identical lido deck. The décor for the newly-fitted public rooms was again the work of the internationally known interior designer Jean Munro and the rooms were also given new names. The forward-facing First Class Bar on Promenade Deck was known as the Parasol Bar and, appropriately, above the circular bar in the centre of the room was a pale pink parasol. The First Class Lounge was renamed the Maple Leaf Room and sported a similar, though generally deeper hued, décor to that in the equivalent room aboard *Carmania*.

***Franconia*'s Caribbean Restaurant had a cool and comfortable look.** *Author's collection.*

The Tourist Class Lounge had become the Mayflower Room and was striking in its primarily red, green and yellow décor. Here, a sweeping, curved staircase led up to the Cactus Club. As on the *Carmania*, this was the most attractive room on the ship, sophisticated and elegant. Its walls were a soft green and it was furnished with chairs and sofas in pale yellow, pale green or coral. The Tourist Class Restaurant now became the Caribbean Restaurant and again the colours pale yellow, coral and green produced a very pleasing effect. To give the room an appropriately tropical feel, the engine-casing that broke up the vastness of the space was covered in a floral wall-covering along with mirrored panels which were draped with a green, red-fringed fabric. The First Class Restaurant was now called the Clock Restaurant and a handsome antique clock adorned the forward wall. While furnished in a similar style to its counterpart aboard *Carmania*, the room had a much more subdued and tasteful colour scheme of coral and black. Altogether, there is little doubt that, although both ships had been fitted out in a very similar style, the décor of *Franconia* was the more elegant.

The transformation had made both ships among the best-equipped cruise ships afloat at that time, able to undertake any length of voyage, and had also made them two of the most attractive liners then serving the North Atlantic. There are, however, some conflicting reports regarding the ultimate cost of refitting them. In *Shipbuilding & Shipping Record*, in April 1963, following the return to service of *Carmania*, it was stated that the work on just that one ship had cost Cunard somewhere in the region of £1 million. More recent accounts on both the line and the ships imply that the refitting of the pair had cost Canard nearer £12 million!

While the conversion had transformed the ships considerably, and was in general met with acclaim, the replacement of their traditional livery of the black hull and white upperworks by Cunard's 'cruising green' rather changed the look of their proportions. It drew one's attention to the fact that the Promenade Deck windows were not full length. This was particularly obvious in relation to the screens sheltering the lido, which did have full length glazing, and thus gave a somewhat off-balance appearance. Considering the extent of the conversions, one is left wondering why the Promenade Deck windows were not re-cut to the appropriate size. This would have enhanced the lines of the ships considerably, giving them a graceful sweep of windows along the full length of the hull, as well as making the enclosed promenade a far more attractive space. It would have improved the view for those passengers who chose to recline in the deckchairs ranged along the promenade, enabling them to see the sea instead of an expanse of white-painted steel.

Toward the end of 1963, having observed the success of the refitting of the first two ships, Cunard announced that both *Carinthia* and *Sylvania* would undergo refits which would enhance their Tourist Class accommodations. Eighty Tourist Class cabins were to be refitted in a style similar to that of the rebuilt ships, giving them private bathrooms as well as new décor. *Carinthia*'s refit was scheduled to take place in Liverpool from the 29th December to the 30th January, 1964; and work on *Sylvania* took place from the 23rd December to the 6th February.

While the upgrading of both ships was doubtless a welcome move, it was far from enough to make them really competitive with other ships then in service or being built. Nor did it address the fact that *Carinthia* and *Sylvania* were, in that trans-Atlantic configuration, quite unsuited to even a seasonal role as cruise ships. To give private bathrooms to eighty Tourist Class appeared to be a token gesture: there were, after all, 250 cabins of that class. Apart from the fact that the passenger facilities did not meet the expectations of the travelling public, the real shortcoming of the Saxonia class was their cargo capacity. It was far too large for liners designed to carry so many passengers – but it was also too small for them to be viable as principally cargo-carriers. The time required to discharge and load cargo is very disruptive for a ship that is also trying to maintain a strict passenger liner schedule. The time it took the four sisters to complete each round trip was far longer than it would have been had they been mainly a passenger operation. On the other hand, in attempting to maintain their passenger schedule, they often missed much lucrative freight. Generally, the cargo carried across to Canada and the United States was very light, often highly-priced, small-quantity goods. Homewards, it was often very similar but with, occasionally, grain and timber also.

Quite simply, in the end the four sisters had not been as successful as Cunard had hoped. Even when faced with that fact, and having transformed *Saxonia* and *Ivernia* into the more cruise-orientated *Carmania* and *Franconia*, the line seemed either unwilling or unable to rebuild the *Carinthia* and *Sylvania* to make them fully compatible with the two earlier ships.

Even Cunard's direct competitors on the U.K. – St. Lawrence run, Canadian Pacific, were beginning to find it difficult to maintain a regular three-ship service by this time. In September, 1963 they withdrew their *Empress of England* from the Atlantic and placed her in full-time cruise service. However, even a two-ship fleet was soon more than they needed and by the end of 1964 they had sold the *Empress of Britain* to Greek Line. Only the splendid and relatively new flagship, *Empress of Canada*, remained as the Saxonia sisters' competitor from the U.K. on the service to the Dominion.

The Cunard Cruising Years

Before *Carmania* re-entered service on the 8th April, 1963, she was inspected by Sir John Brocklebank at Southampton. He was said to be "overjoyed" to see how the ship had undergone such a transformation. Despite being rebuilt with the cruise market very squarely in mind, *Carmania* immediately returned to service on the regular North Atlantic run. On the 25th May, *Franconia*, her refitting completed, left Glasgow on a trial voyage and arrived at Southampton on the 30th. Two days later, she also resumed the Atlantic service with calls at Rotterdam and Le Havre en route to Quebec. Initial sailings via Rotterdam by both ships were quite successful and it seemed for some while that all was going very well for the revitalised liners. In October, after she had been back in service for six months, *Carmania* was greeted by violent scenes at Quebec when she arrived during a dockworkers' strike. One of her crewmembers received a gunshot wound during the incident.

***Franconia*, in her early green livery, at anchor in the Caribbean.** *Captain Ron Warwick collection.*

While, later that year, *Carmania* settled into her first programme of winter cruises from Port Everglades, *Franconia* made her Caribbean debut with a series of cruises out of New York. She departed on the first of these on the 23rd November, sailing to St. Thomas, Santo Domingo, Kingston and Nassau. A series of similar cruises continued until the 24th April, 1964, when she sailed for Southampton to join *Carmania* in the summer trans-Atlantic service.

It was at this time that Cunard were beginning to see that there was a need to turn more of their attention towards the cruise market. So, along with the *Carmania* and *Franconia*, other members of the fleet, more usually seen on the Atlantic run, were sent on rather experimental cruises. They included the legendary *Queen Mary* and *Queen Elizabeth*, as well as the glorious *Mauretania* – though she had maintained a regular winter Caribbean cruise programme since her return from war service in 1947. These ships were, however, still essentially trans-Atlantic liners and were without the facilities that passengers were beginning to expect more and more on a ship cruising the tropics. Even despite their recent upgrading, the *Carinthia* and *Sylvania* fell far short of those expectations. At that time, in the mid-1960s, when the number of passengers travelling across the Atlantic by sea had fallen to approximately 600,000 per annum, Cunard could really only boast a fleet of three cruise ships and one of those, the *Caronia*, fabulous though she was, represented a style of travel from another age. She, although the doyenne of the grand cruise circuit, was being seriously challenged by more modern yet still very elegant ships like Norway's *Bergensfjord*, Sweden's *Gripsholm* and the soon to be introduced *Sagafjord* and *Kungsholm*.

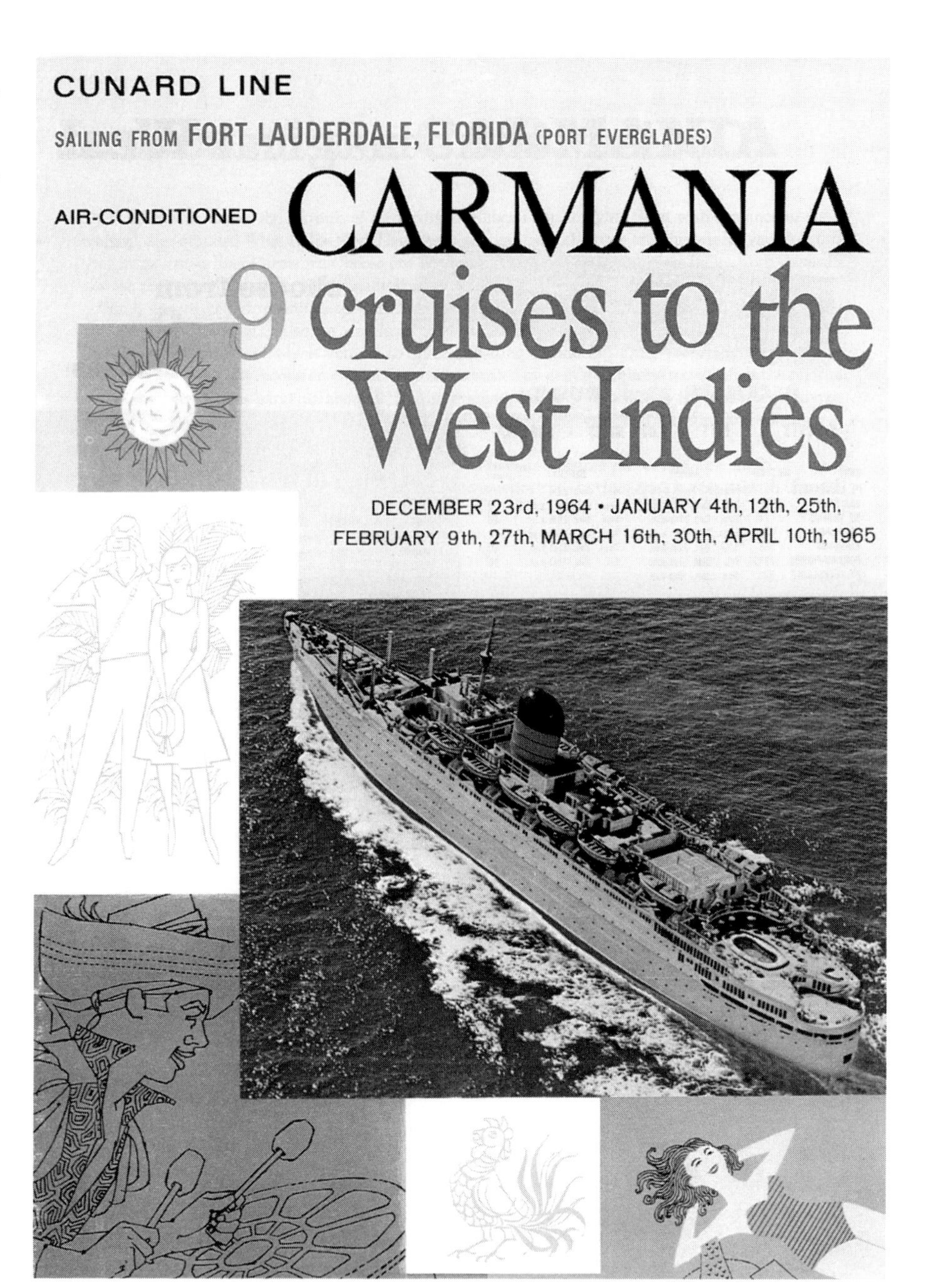

Captain Ron Warwick collection.

By the winter of 1964/65, both *Carmania* and *Franconia* were well-established on the cruise scene and on the 23rd December *Carmania* departed Port Everglades on a 3,033 mile Christmas and New Year's cruise that took her to five ports: San Juan, St. Thomas, Curaçao, Kingston and Port au Prince. It was the first in a programme of nine cruises which would vary in length from 6 to 17 days. *Franconia*, meanwhile, continued with the programme that she had established the previous winter, sailing out of New York to the Caribbean. She operated six cruises, the first one departing New York on the 8th December, 1964. Due to the extra sailing time required to reach the warm Caribbean, her cruises were a little longer than those of her sister, being of 10, 12, 13, 15 or 19 days duration.

It is interesting to note the 'Hints For Packing' in a cruise brochure of this period. Instead of playing down any requirement for formal dressing, as is so usual now, the potential passenger was instructed "You'll dress for dinner except the first and last nights out or when the ship leaves a port in the late afternoon, which means you'll want a wardrobe of evening wear... a fur cape or stole will be in order over your very dressiest evening gowns or cocktail dresses... for the men, may we suggest miracle-fabric business suits, a supply of dress shirts, slacks and sports shirts and formal wear of tropical weight."

Franconia arrived back in Southampton on the 1st April, 1965 and underwent an overhaul and refit before resuming her schedule of trans-Atlantic crossings to Canada on the 13th, with most departures including Rotterdam. On the 1st October that year, she ventured into the Mediterranean for the very first time. Cunard had scheduled her to undertake an Iberian cruise, departing Southampton on the 25th September and calling at Malaga, Cadiz, Lisbon and Pauillac. She followed this with a similar cruise, which called at Casablanca instead of Malaga. A further sailing was made to Canada and then she returned to New York for another season of six Caribbean cruises, which ran from the 20th December to the 20th March, 1966. *Carmania*'s cruise programme that winter began on the 22nd December and continued until the 17th April, 1966.

Meanwhile, *Carinthia* and *Sylvania* had continued with their year-round trans-Atlantic service. *Carinthia*'s 27th December, 1964 arrival in New York had caused problems. The dockworkers went on strike over the berth that she had been allocated and as a result her return voyage departure was delayed until the 2nd January, 1965.

By this time, it had become apparent to the directors of Cunard that the demand for trans-Atlantic voyages during mid-winter was declining rapidly and the decision was taken to send both *Carinthia* and *Sylvania* off on a series of winter cruises, even though they were not fully suited to cruising. It fell to the *Sylvania* to initiate these and she sailed from Liverpool on the 10th February, 1965 on what was, in fact, only the second cruise of her career – a fabulous 27-day odyssey into the Mediterranean, calling at Gibraltar, Naples, Piraeus, Alexandria, Beirut, Haifa, Messina and Lisbon. She also made a Christmas cruise from Liverpool, leaving on the 22nd December for Madeira, Tenerife, Las Palmas, Casablanca and Gibraltar. On the 7th January, 1966 *Carinthia* sailed from Liverpool on the same itinerary. Two days after her return, she departed on a similar cruise of 13 nights before returning to her more usual winter service on the Liverpool – New York run. After her Christmas cruise, *Sylvania* sailed for Southampton, arriving there for the very first time on the 26th January, 1966. On the 28th, she left on a cruise to the Atlantic islands, Casablanca and Lisbon and followed it with a month-long cruise into the Mediterranean. She then made two shorter trips, one to the Atlantic islands and the other taking her once more into the Mediterranean, before resuming her trans-Atlantic service to New York on the 20th April.

In early May, 1966, Britain was hit by the National Seamen's Strike. This was to have a devastating effect, practically bringing all the ports round the country to a standstill and virtually immobilising many lines. The strike dragged on for over six weeks, not ending until the 1st July. Ports such as Southampton presented an incredible sight. Never had so many liners been gathered together in one place at the same time. In some instances they were berthed three abreast. All four of the 'sisters' were caught by the strike action. *Carmania*, having left Port Everglades on the 19th April on an Atlantic crossing to Southampton via Nassau, Bermuda and Le Havre, arrived in time to be one of the early victims. *Franconia*, barely a month into her Atlantic season, also became strikebound in the port's Eastern Docks. Both *Carinthia* and *Sylvania* were stopped in Liverpool. So, for several weeks, there was no Cunard Line service across the Atlantic to either New York or Canada. With this most prestigious player temporarily out of the game, it was left to the liners of Holland America, Norddeutscher Lloyd, French Line and the United States Lines to fill the void. By mid-July, however, all was returned to normal, but so many weeks with its entire fleet inactive had an unfortunate effect on the finances of the Cunard Line.

On her return to service, *Carinthia* was involved in a couple of minor incidents. She damaged one of her propellers while she was in Montreal harbour in August and had to undergo repairs on her return to Liverpool. Then, on the 25th October, she collided with the vessel *Forester* while in Liverpool. But 1966 ended on an even more dramatic note for her. On the 8th December, she was caught in the worst gale of her career, which caused her to arrive in Liverpool two days late. The storm damage necessitated a dry-docking, which included work on her badly injured rudder. Cunard had planned to repaint the ship all-white in time for her Christmas cruise but the delay caused by the storm and the time spent on repairs meant that no time was available for this additional change to her appearance. She kept her black hull not just for the Christmas cruise but also for the rest of her career with Cunard.

Her 14-night Christmas cruise departed Liverpool on the 23rd December and took the traditional route to the Atlantic islands, Gibraltar and Lisbon.

Carinthia returned to Liverpool on the 6th January, 1967. The year was to prove the most significant since her entry into service. Having made one trans-Atlantic crossing to Halifax and New York, she sailed for Southampton and undertook another Atlantic islands cruise. There were two more crossings to New York before the resumption of the Liverpool – Canada service but on the 20th July *Carinthia* sailed from the Mersey on a cruise to Lisbon, Cadiz, Casablanca and Vigo. This was followed by another, similar but including Madeira instead of Cadiz. This was to be her very last cruise under the Cunard house flag. However, at the time this fact was perhaps known only to the most important people in the company. She made a further six round-trip crossings to Canada.

Unlike *Carinthia, Sylvania* did have her black hull repainted white, during her annual refit and overhaul in December, 1966. Cunard had planned an extensive programme of cruises for her, somewhat more imaginative than had been operated by the other ships. These were to keep her busy during the whole winter and through until early May, 1967. On the 13th January, she left Southampton on what was her most glamorous cruise: 36 days to the Caribbean. It was a far cry from her normal winter employment battling to and from New York, often in those latter years with as few as two or three hundred passengers only. Now, she headed south to Las Palmas and then on the southerly route to Trinidad, Barbados, Fort de France, Antigua, St. Thomas, San Juan, Nassau, Port Everglades, Bermuda and back to Southampton via Madeira. At that time, many of those ports still had the allure of being exotic and relatively untouched by mass tourism.

On her return, *Sylvania* made news when Cunard announced that she would be equipped with an SRN-6 hovercraft. Carried on her foredeck, it was to be used to take cruise passengers on sightseeing excursions during the following programme of cruises. This was in part an experiment to study the practicalities of giving other ships similar hovercraft. It appears, however, that it did not meet with much success or popularity as no hovercraft were fitted aboard other cruise ships. *Sylvania* left Southampton on the 23rd February, 1967, complete with hovercraft, for a Mediterranean cruise. This was unusual at the time, yet a precursor of things to come, in that the voyage ended at Gibraltar and the passengers were flown home from there. A further four Mediterranean cruises followed, with the passengers being flown out to Gibraltar. The last of these sailed from Gibraltar on the 18th April for Malaga, Famagusta, Beirut, Haifa, Naples, Messina and Lisbon and returned to Southampton on the 10th May. Although *Sylvania* was hardly appropriate as a cruise ship, it suddenly seemed that Cunard had begun fully to appreciate the need to cater for this growing market. This series of winter and spring cruises had shown some imagination and diversity. Sadly, it was to prove to be too little too late.

Shortly after her return to Southampton, *Sylvania* reverted to her Atlantic service to Quebec and Montreal. On the 15th June, in the early stages of a return voyage, she ran aground off Trois Rivières. There appeared to be no damage but she was stuck fast and efforts to refloat her were unsuccessful. On the 17th, it was decided that she should be lightened by disembarking all passengers and pumping her bunkers into barges. She was finally refloated the following day and on the 19th returned to Montreal. However, it was not until the 26th that she was dry-docked and there must have been some hull damage because she remained in the dock until the 29th. She was not ready to resume her aborted voyage until the 4th July.

The year 1967 must be recorded in the annals of Cunard history perhaps as both the most depressing and yet the most hopeful. The new superliner "Q4" was now under construction – but on the 8th May, the Chairman, Sir Basil Smallpiece, announced that the legendary "Queens" were to be withdrawn earlier than had been initially expected. *Queen Mary* was to be retired that autumn and *Queen Elizabeth*, which had been scheduled for a life-extending refit that would make her a fitting running-mate for the new ship, would instead be withdrawn in the autumn of 1968. A further blow came in October, the very month that saw the final voyage of *Queen Mary*, when the directors of Cunard came to a decision that would have further repercussions through the fleet and which would shock both the shipping world and the travelling public alike. The prestigious, but hugely expensive, *Caronia* was to be withdrawn from service. The line had lost £2 million during the first six months of the year. As a result, they were unwilling to invest any more money in making the sister ships *Carinthia* and *Sylvania* suitable for cruising. They too would be placed on the market, for sale, and Sir Basil stated that the company were willing to let them go "with no strings attached".

Carinthia sailed from Southampton on the 23rd November for her final voyage across the Atlantic under the Cunard flag. This last voyage did not take her into the St. Lawrence as by now the winter ice had become a hazard. Instead, she docked at Halifax and sailed from there on the 3rd December. Six days later, she was back in Southampton and her career as a Cunarder was at an end. She was laid up alongside *Caronia*, which had been withdrawn the previous month.

Sylvania was to be a little luckier in that the refit she had undergone earlier in the year ensured her career in the company's service for almost six months more. She sailed from Southampton on her last trip to Montreal on the 20th October but returned to Liverpool. It was from there that she left for her last Atlantic crossing on the 30th November, but to New York instead of Canada. She sailed via Cobh and Halifax and also called at these ports on the homeward voyage. She arrived back in Southampton on the 20th and two days later she left on a Christmas cruise to Lisbon, Madeira, Tenerife, Casablanca, Gibraltar and Cadiz. *Sylvania*'s remaining months under the Cunard flag were spent as a cruise ship. On the 10th January, 1968, she sailed on a month-long voyage out to the Caribbean. From the end of February through to early May, she undertook a series of cruises that were very similar to those of the previous year in that she sailed out to the Atlantic islands with the first cruise ending at Gibraltar. The remaining six cruises were based there and included several ports in the Mediterranean. Her final Cunard cruise departed Gibraltar on the 24th April and called at Barcelona, Naples, Palma and Lisbon, ending at Southampton on the 7th May. She was then laid up alongside her sister *Carinthia* and the *Caronia* at berth 101. They were redundant, outmoded – yet, ironically, the sisters' most successful years were still to come.

While the Cunard careers of both *Carinthia* and *Sylvania* were at an end, the other pair, *Carmania* and *Franconia* continued to maintain the company's cruise programme, as well as a much-reduced summer liner service to Canada. Cruising was, however, to become the most important part of their employment. In fact,

Franconia would, in 1967, become a full-time cruise ship. In 1966, the Furness-Bermuda Line withdrew their two ships, *Queen of Bermuda* and *Ocean Monarch*, from the cruise service between New York and Bermuda. The line was well-established and the two splendid ships were very much a part of the waterfront scenes at both New York and Hamilton, Bermuda. They had loyal followings but would have required considerable work to bring them into line with stringent new safety requirements then coming into force. Faced with the expense of this work and with the advanced age of *Queen of Bermuda*, Furness-Bermuda Line had decided to cease operations. Cunard saw that the gap the withdrawal would leave as an ideal opportunity to establish themselves in the year-round cruise market out of the United States. Arrangements were made with the Bermudan government for *Franconia* to become the weekly cruise ship between New York and the island.

Cunard had, however, already begun to send the ships on somewhat more diverse itineraries and on the 1st October, 1966 *Carmania* made her first Mediterranean cruise before returning to her usual winter employment in the Caribbean. It was at this time, during their winter refits, that both *Carmania* and *Franconia* underwent a further change: their "cruising green" livery was dispensed with in favour of the more conventional white hull and upperworks. As before, *Carmania* was based in Port Everglades but for part of this 1966/67 season she was joined there by *Franconia*, which had in the past sailed to the Caribbean from New York. *Franconia* had made a 10-day Christmas and New Year cruise out of New York, returning there on the 2nd January. The following day, she sailed for Nassau and Port Everglades and then into the Caribbean, returning to the Florida port. She made three subsequent cruises from there but with the last one, a 19-day trip, she returned to New York.

It was on the 23rd March, 1967 that *Franconia* sailed

Carmania glistening in the sunlight, at anchor in the Mediterranean. *Captain Ron Warwick collection*

Later in her career, *Franconia*, seen here at New York, was painted white. *Donald Stoltenberg.*

from New York on the first of a planned series of 28 cruises to Bermuda. She did, however, make one diversion from this regular route when, on the 18th July, she sailed northwards to what had once been her customary trading area, the St. Lawrence River. This cruise took her from New York to Quebec, Montreal and Boston, ending in Bermuda. She then made a second cruise to Montreal and Quebec, this time ending in New York. This allowed her to resume her regular Bermuda schedule. The series of cruises to Bermuda ended on the 17th November and three days later *Franconia* sailed for Liverpool via Bermuda and Cobh. This was her first Atlantic voyage of the year. She remained at Liverpool, being overhauled, until the 22nd December when she departed on a Christmas cruise to the Atlantic islands and North Africa.

While 1967 had seen *Franconia* experiencing her first year as a full-time cruise ship, *Carmania* was employed in her final season as a trans-Atlantic liner. Her final sailing in this mode started at Montreal on the 26th September. However, she had made a four-day cruise from Montreal and Quebec on the 8th August, undoubtedly a farewell gesture, and it was fitting that the lead ship of the quartet should have made it. An era had ended.

Carmania returned to Southampton and once again made a Mediterranean cruise. It was 19 days long and, unlike the previous year's cruise which only called at western Mediterranean ports, this time went as far as Istanbul. The winter months were, as usual, spent in the Caribbean. 1968 would be her first year as a full-time cruise ship. Cunard had planned an extensive European programme for her, which took her into quite unfamiliar waters. On the 18th June, for example, she sailed from Southampton on her first excursion into Scandinavian waters. The itinerary seems, in these days of rather more port-intensive cruises, to have been quite remarkable – not so much for the ports which the ship visited as for those she did not - she called at Rotterdam, Bergen, Hammerfest, Copenhagen and Hamburg. Other trips took her to the more familiar areas of the Atlantic islands, Spain, Portugal and Morocco. On the 28th September, *Carmania* began a programme of fly-cruises. She first sailed into the Mediterranean, ending at Naples, and her passengers were flown home from there. There followed a series of four cruises, all based on Naples, which included such exciting ports as Venice, Rhodes and Dubrovnik. The final cruise of the series ended back in Southampton in November.

That winter, *Carmania* returned to the Caribbean. Her

cruise programme proved to be a memorable one – not, however, in a way that would please Cunard. The Christmas cruise had to be cancelled, disappointing hundreds of potential passengers, when it appeared that the ship was in contravention of the US fire regulations. Modifications were made and finished in time for her to meet the departure date for her next cruise, scheduled for the 11th January, 1969. On the afternoon of the very next day, she ran aground on a sandbank one mile west of San Salvador in the Bahamas. She was stuck so firmly that it was five days before she could be refloated. By that time, of course, the rest of her 12-day cruise had been cancelled and her passengers had been taken to Miami. By a strange coincidence, they had been transferred onto the Italian ship *Flavia*, which in earlier days had been the Cunard combination cargo/passenger liner *Media* and was therefore a former fleet-mate of *Carmania*. Once refloated, *Carmania* was moved into the lee of Eleuthera Island, where she was inspected by divers. Not surprisingly, her hull was found to be damaged and she was sent to the shipyards at Newport News, Virginia to be repaired. The work took almost a month and she did not resume her schedule until the 8th February. An enquiry was held and it transpired that there had been a fault in the Admiralty charts for the area.

Just three months later, *Carmania* was in trouble again. On the 12th May, she collided off Gibraltar with the Russian ship *Frunze* and damaged her bow. Temporary repairs were made and she resumed her cruise programme five days later. While 1968 had seen *Carmania* make her first cruise to Norway, in 1969 she made her first cruise to the capitals of the Baltic. This was followed by a further series of Mediterranean cruises based on Naples and the winter of 1969/70 saw her back, as usual, in the Caribbean.

Meanwhile, during the greater part of 1968, from mid-April to November, *Franconia* had again maintained the regular cruise service linking New York and Bermuda. Before that, she had begun the year with a cruise from Liverpool to Portugal, North Africa and the Atlantic islands before sailing over to New York to make three cruises down to the Caribbean. In late November, after the end of the Bermuda season, she was back in Southampton where she underwent a month-long refit and overhaul before sailing on her usual Christmas and New Year cruise. The itinerary was slightly different this time, for in addition to the usual Atlantic islands and North African ports of call, Dakar in Senegal was also included.

Franconia forsook New York in favour of Florida as the base for her winter cruise programme of 1969. On the 8th January, she left Southampton for Miami and made a cruise from there to San Juan and St. Thomas. The cruise ended in Port Everglades and the remainder of the cruise programme was based on that port. The pattern of *Franconia*'s employment for the year 1969 was virtually identical with that of previous years – early April to mid-November sailing between New York and Bermuda and back in Southampton by the end of the month in time for refitting. That year, her Christmas and New Year cruise was scheduled so that she was in Madeira on the 31st December so that her passengers could witness the famous and spectacular fireworks display.

The year 1969 had seen developments that would have far-reaching effects on the futures of both *Carmania* and *Franconia*. The Overseas National Airways Company of New York had placed an order with the Rotterdam Drydock Company for a 14,155 gross ton cruise ship. The original order carried an option for two further ships and they were intended to fit into Overseas National's proposed fly-cruise programme to the Caribbean. In 1970, inspired by the success of *Carmania* and *Franconia*'s cruises in the area, Cunard took a 50% interest in the operation and a new joint company, Cunard-ONA, was formed to own and operate the first ship. The option for the second ship was taken up at this time. Three months later, in July 1970, Overseas National Airways were forced to withdraw from the arrangement, thwarted by various US regulations. This left Cunard in sole possession of one partially completed ship plus the option for a second, scheduled for delivery in 1972.

Before embarking on this ill-fated joint venture, Cunard had given thought to replacing *Carmania* and *Franconia* with their first-ever purpose-built cruise ships which would have been of about 24,000 gross tons. Given the ultimate lack of success of the ships which became *Cunard Adventurer* and *Cunard Ambassador*, it is perhaps unfortunate that they did not follow this course of action. Most of Cunard's problems at this time had resulted from operating too big passenger ships, designed originally as trans-Atlantic liners, with too high a passenger/crew ratio and too low a degree of luxury to live up to the reputation of the line. However, at the time *Cunard Adventurer* was due to enter service – in mid-November, 1971 – it was questioned in industry circles whether she was, in fact, too small. Certainly, judging by the standards of other ships operating at that time she seemed small indeed, particularly when one considers that she could accommodate as many as 806 passengers.

Cunard had taken over the Overseas National contract for the two ships for £16 million and with subsequent design alterations this rose to £20 million. It was a high price when one considers that in 1967 Sir Basil Smallpiece had announced that, with £2 million losses in the first half of the year, the line was unwilling to put more money into making *Carinthia* and *Sylvania* viable as cruise ships. *Shipbuilding & Shipping Record* reported in December, 1971 that "... it was wrong and unfair to compare her (*Cunard Adventurer*) with previous Cunarders." They further noted that the exterior design of the new ship had been the responsibility of James Gardner, one of the *Queen Elizabeth 2*'s design co-ordinators. Mr. Gardner apparently had in mind the style of a luxury yacht when designing *Cunard Adventurer*. Order and unity were the results he was striving for. *Shipbuilding & Shipping Record* reported, in somewhat cutting tones, "We think he has failed... there is little scope on a ship of *Cunard*

Adventurer's size to provide a feeling of spaciousness either in the indoor public areas or open upper decks... the result, it must be said, is disappointing..." These were comments that were a far cry from the praise that was accorded the former *Saxonia* and *Ivernia* when they emerged from John Brown's as *Carmania* and *Franconia*. It was, however, against this backdrop of a £20 million investment in two inappropriate ships that *Carmania* and *Franconia* would be sacrificed.

By this time, both ships had built up a loyal following and were very popular on both sides of the Atlantic. Early in 1970, their port of registry was changed from Liverpool to Southampton. However, as Cunard was still facing considerable financial problems related to the costs of both fuel and crews, it might have been better had they taken the money-saving route of adopting flags of convenience. It is possible that it was considered, but with the crippling seamen's strike of 1966 still clearly in memory, flags of convenience may not have really been an option for the line. So they were faced with the fact that, even with a full complement of passengers, it was possible for the ships to lose money.

During the summer of 1970, *Carmania* undertook a full programme of cruises out of Southampton. On the 10th December, she made a trans-Atlantic crossing to New York, but en route to Port Everglades for her usual winter programme. It was her first arrival in New York as *Carmania. Franconia* joined her in January. Sadly, it was to be their last season in the Caribbean.

In 1971, Cunard suddenly found themselves facing the most important event of their long and illustrious history – a take-over bid. First, there came an attempted take-over by the hotel group Grand Metropolitan. This was followed in August by a successful bid that shocked the shipping world. This time it came, at £26 million, from Trafalgar House Investments, Ltd., a company with interests in property, civil engineering, hotel ownership, house building and investments. The question on everyone's lips at that time was "what can they possibly know about shipping?" What they did not know, they had to learn, and quickly, in order to return the line to a more healthy and profitable state.

They were faced with the fact that both *Carmania* and *Franconia* were in need of further refitting and modernisation. With several new purpose-built cruise ships coming into the market, the two sisters were beginning to look dated, particularly when compared with their new fleetmates, the striking flagship *Queen Elizabeth*

The Sale Prospectus for *Franconia* and *Carmania*. *Author's collection.*

H. E. MOSS & COMPANY LIMITED

EXCLUSIVELY IN OUR HANDS FOR SALE UNDER INSTRUCTIONS FROM CUNARD LINE LTD.

R.M.S. "FRANCONIA" — R.M.S. "CARMANIA"

R.M.S. "Carmania"

2 and the cruise ship *Cunard Adventurer*. Cunard, and their new masters, Trafalgar House, realised that to bring *Carmania* and *Franconia* up to standard would be an expensive business. They approached several British shipyards for estimates and even asked the Greek shipping line Chandris, who had their own ship repair facility, to undertake the work. Plans were drawn up which would have involved selling the ships to Chandris, with Cunard still acting as managers. However, nothing came of the plan or of the other options to refit the pair. Instead, it was decided that they should be withdrawn from service, laid up and offered for sale. Their roles in the Caribbean would be filled by the new cruise ships *Cunard Adventurer* and *Cunard Ambassador*.

***Franconia* and *Carmania* and Shaw Savill's *Southern Cross* laid up in the King Harry Reach of the River Fal in Cornwall.**
Alan Kittridge collection.

Meanwhile, both ships soldiered on. *Franconia* maintained her regular pattern of sailings, with Caribbean cruises in the winter and then on the New York to Bermuda run throughout the Summer. She departed New York on the 2nd October, 1971 on her final cruise to Bermuda. Her last sailing for Cunard was a trans-Atlantic voyage on which she left New York, never to return, on the 9th October. It was not to be a run-of-the-mill voyage: when she was part way across the Atlantic, she responded to a distress call from the burning Norwegian bulk carrier *Anatina*. Using one of her launches, *Franconia* was able to take off eight of the crew from the burning ship. She arrived in Southampton on the 17th October, her career under the Cunard flag at an end.

Carmania's final season was a programme of eight cruises out of Southampton to the Mediterranean, based on Naples. Her final Cunard cruise departed Naples on the 24th October and she was back at Southampton on the 31st. She was placed in lay up, alongside *Franconia*, which had arrived two weeks earlier. A few days later, they were joined by the Shaw Savill liner *Southern Cross*, that had also been withdrawn from service. The three redundant liners made a majestic, yet sad sight at the berth, awaiting their fate.

Carmania and *Franconia* remained there for almost seven months. When it was apparent that there was no immediate prospect of selling them, Cunard decided to place them in more permanent lay up and on the 14th May, 1972 the two ships sailed for the River Fal in Cornwall. At one time, Toyo Yusen of Japan seemed a likely buyer and then the famous shipping magnate C. Y. Tung showed some interest. However, no offer was received from either of them and Cunard continued to explore other possibilities of employment for the ships. It was costing £10,000 per month to keep them laid up in the River Fal and they were losing value through deterioration and obsolescence. In late 1972, Cunard evaluated the possibility of returning *Franconia* to service in 1973/74. The proposal was to operate her from Norfolk, Virginia to Bermuda or Nassau and the Caribbean in the summer and between Recife and Montevideo in the winter. However, it was realised that the high cost of returning the ship to operational standard was far more than that of keeping her laid up.

Details of the pair were again circulated to all the London-based shipbrokers. Also during 1972, Cunard contacted the fledgling Norwegian Caribbean Line to explore the possibility of chartering *Franconia* to them to replace their *Sunward*, which they had recently sold. It was a desperate move: Norwegian Caribbean were rapidly expanding with purpose-built cruise ships designed specifically for the Caribbean and it must have been unlikely that they would want an outdated former Atlantic liner as part of their fleet. Of course, in time that is exactly what they did acquire, when they purchased *France* in 1979. But in the early 1970s, former trans-Atlantic liners were not in high demand, so the future looked bleak for the once-glamorous Cunarders. It is also interesting to note that in time, NCL would acquire one of the ships that hastened the departure of *Carmania* and *Franconia* from the Cunard fleet – the *Cunard Adventurer*. As *Sunward II*, she would, in fact, be for NCL a far more successful ship than she ever was with Cunard.

The Sisters Separate

Carinthia and *Sylvania* were destined to spend over two years lying idle at Southampton's Berth 101. Yet interest in them, even though they had very little in the way of cruise facilities to make them attractive to potential buyers, came much more quickly than was to be the case with their more cruise-orientated sisters. On the 31st January, 1968 a contract for their sale was signed in London. The pair had been bought for just £1 million each and the buyers were reported to be the Fairland Shipping Corporation and the Fairwind Shipping Corporation. *Carinthia* was to be renamed *Fairland* and *Sylvania* would become *Fairwind*, but they would, in fact, be sailing for the Sitmar Line, Italian-based but controlled from Monaco. The sale, which was completed on the 2nd February, included a clause which prevented the two ships from operating on any of Cunard's regular routes, such as those from the United Kingdom to either Canada or the US east coast ports. They were also precluded from sailing on cruises from British ports.

Società Italiana Trasporti Marittimi SpA, otherwise known as the Sitmar Line, had been formed in 1938 by Alexandre Vlasov. He was a White Russian, born of Cossack parents in 1880 – strange and romantic beginnings for a man who would go on to found one of the most important and influential passenger ship operations in the World. For many years, Sitmar Line was involved in the Australian migrant and low-fare around-the-World tourist trades. Some of the vessels used had originally been C3-type escort carriers and others had been wartime-built 'Victory' ships that had served as troop transports. Much rebuilt by Sitmar, they had become very serviceable emigrant-carriers. By the late 1960s, however, the line had disposed of several of their older ships and were looking for higher-quality vessels with which to maintain their service between northern Europe and Australia. At the time, they had the Australian government contract to carry migrants from Southampton out to Australia, so the two redundant Cunarders appeared to fit their requirements exactly and would have made fine fleet-mates to the company's *Fairstar*, the former Bibby troopship *Oxfordshire*.

Having given the two ships names well-suited to vessels carrying emigrants out to new lives in a young country, the new owners seemed to do nothing with them other than repaint the funnels in their colours, buff with a large blue V (for Vlasov). The fact was that almost as soon as Sitmar had bought *Carinthia* and *Sylvania* the Australian government, instead of renewing their contract, awarded it to the Chandris Line. So Sitmar had either to attempt eventually to regain it – which they hoped to do with ambitious plans to convert the Cunarders into two of the finest migrant ships ever – or to find an alternative use for them. Without that valuable contract there was no way that the ships could be operated profitably on the Australian run. Thus, *Fairland* and *Fairwind* sat, looking somewhat forlorn, becoming a feature of the Southampton waterfront as Sitmar worked on other ways of employing them. It was becoming ever more obvious that the migrant contract would remain with Chandris and that by the time it ended, airplanes would take over.

Boris Vlasov, who had taken command of Sitmar on the death of his father in 1961, set the project in motion: code name 'Concarsyl', short for 'Conversion of *Carinthia* and *Sylvania*'. The plan was to rebuild them totally into de luxe cruise ships and tenders for the work were requested from several European shipyards. Meanwhile, Sitmar developed a new plan of employment for them, still with Australia very much in mind. They were to be based in Los Angeles and would sail to San Francisco and Vancouver before crossing the Pacific on what would have been the most exotic of liner voyages – lasting a month, it would have called at Honolulu, Papeete, Raitea, Pago Pago and Suva before arriving in Auckland and then across to Sydney. After about three months of cruising out of Sydney, a return voyage would be made to California. Cruises were also scheduled out of Los Angeles. While one ship would be cruising from Sydney, the other would be doing the same from Los Angeles.

The trans-Pacific voyages were due to begin in May, 1972 and literature was produced and the marketing was put into effect. Some of the voyages were to include additional ports such as Lautoka, Niuafo'ou Island and Apia. It is interesting to see in that early brochure that the line actually acknowledged the interest – indeed, the existence – of ship enthusiasts. They advised that "We wish to advise passengers that prior to the arrival at Los Angeles from Sydney, or after departure Los Angeles for Sydney, the vessel will dry-dock in San Francisco. You may use it as your hotel whilst sightseeing in San Francisco and although there will be maintenance work and repainting in progress during this time, you will not be disturbed in your room and the inconvenience will be minimal. Most ship enthusiasts find the dry-dock stay a fascinating experience."

From the earliest design stages of the conversion, considerable attention was given to safety. Arthur Crook, who was Lloyd's Register's senior surveyor in charge of Passenger Ship Safety Certification at the time, was seconded to the Sitmar headquarters in Monaco. There he worked alongside the company's naval architect, Dario Rivera, establishing layouts and safety standards for the vessels. After preliminary conversion plans had been produced, various European shipyards were contacted for estimates. Having previously had good experience of working with Arsenale Triestino – San Marco of Trieste, Mr. Crook recommended that yard and ultimately the contract for the conversions was awarded to them. Both they and Sitmar agreed to apply 1948 Safety of Life at Sea (SOLAS) regulations, which included a sprinkler system throughout the ship. But they also agreed, at Mr. Crook's suggestion, that all corridor bulkheads should be of B-class standard and should extend from deck to deck, thus providing at least 30 minutes safe exit in case of fire. Subsequently, it was possible to have the ships comply fully with 1960 SOLAS regulations with the application of certain down-flooding techniques in order to satisfy damage stability requirements. At that time, cruise ship companies were obliged by American law (later rescinded) to state in their advertising which SOLAS regulations they complied with, either as a 'new' or 'existing' ship. Having been so closely involved with the design stages of the two vessels, Mr. Crook then spent considerable time at the shipyard in Trieste as the work of rebuilding got underway.

On the 6th January, 1970, *Fairwind* left Southampton under tow and arrived at Trieste on the 18th January. She was joined by *Fairland* on the 21st February. While both ships were being completely rebuilt, Sitmar continued trying to market their proposed Pacific liner service and cruises. Sitmar Cruises, Inc. was established by the line, purely to operate the two ships. Despite their attempts to attract passengers in both Australia and the United States, Sitmar found they could not arouse sufficient interest among the travelling public, particularly for the trans-Pacific voyages. Long-haul Pacific cruises out of Los Angeles and San Francisco were at that time totally the domain of *Mariposa* and *Monterey*. They were well-established vessels, having sailed for Matson Line for several years, and had now been taken over by Pacific Far East Line, who were continuing to operate them in the same service. Meanwhile, the mighty P&O empire was well entrenched in Australia and had several large liners employed on Pacific routes. In addition, lines such as Shaw Savill and Lloyd Triestino were also well-known on other trans-Pacific routes. While Sitmar were known in Australia and could perhaps have attracted some business, it would not have been enough to make the liner service viable. However, while they were still totally unknown in the United States, they had aroused some interest in the cruise programme, enough to encourage them to re-think the way in which they might employ the ships.

Boris Vlasov felt that, with the transportation of migrants a thing of the past, the only real future for the company lay in cruising. But despite having established the Liberian-based Sitmar Cruises, Inc. to operate the two new ships, the line had at that time very little experience of cruise service. Once in a while, they had sent their *Fairsky*, *Fairstar* and *Castel Felice* cruising out of Sydney to some of the Pacific islands. *Fairstar* had, indeed, achieved some success in this role and, each December and January since 1966, had been diverted from her liner service to northern Europe in order to carry out a short programme of cruises. Otherwise, such diversions from their normal employment had been rare for the Sitmar ships. It was, therefore, a bold decision for the line to market the new vessels purely as cruise ships.

Despite the disappointing response to the trans-Pacific venture and the fact that Sitmar was all but unknown in America, Boris Vlasov was convinced that this was where the future lay. The American cruise market was then showing considerable potential for growth and he made the decision to base both ships year round in Los Angeles: cruising to Mexico in the winter and up to Alaska in the summer. It was a decision that ultimately made a huge impact on the US cruise market and that ensured immense popularity and lengthy lives for the ships.

The conversion of *Fairland* and *Fairwind* was little short of remarkable and was reported to have cost $56 million. The two ships sat in adjacent berths at the Arsenale Triestino yard while much of their superstructure was cut away and their interiors were stripped out. In April, 1970, *Fairland* was renamed. That original name, which had seemed so suitable for an emigrant-carrying vessel, no longer suited her new and infinitely more glamorous role as a cruise ship. Thus, she was re-christened *Fairsea*. She was the first of the pair to be completed and emerged from the yard looking utterly different from her former self as the Cunarder *Carinthia*. Gone were the cargo-handling derricks; gone was that unmistakable domed funnel; gone were the enclosed promenades. All that one could see that hinted at her former life was the shape of her hull and its distinctive stern anchor. Internally, all passenger and officer spaces had been removed and the ship had been taken down to the bare steel to enable the transformation to be achieved under the guidance of the famous Italian architect Umberto Nordio. The staid-looking Cunarder became an elegant Italian cruise ship. Her superstructure now extended forward and was completed by a gracefully curved and enlarged bridgefront. What had been an enclosed promenade from which to view the cold North Atlantic had been opened up to allow passengers to enjoy the tropical sea breezes. The greatest change, however, was aft. Here, instead of cargo hatches, derricks and the aft docking bridge, there were tiered sun decks, lido areas and three pools, one of which was just for children. Instead of the massive funnel, the ship now sported a handsomely raked one, perhaps a little more conventional but, with its stylish smoke-deflecting fin, well-suited to her new look. *Fairsea* was resplendent in her new all-white livery, with just three short blue stripes at her bow and the uppermost decks painted the same shade of buff as her funnel. To complete the look of a brand new ship, 25 tons of dented hull plates had been renewed.

While *Fairsea* cut a rakish figure with her Italian styling, she nevertheless still had the overall look of a traditional liner of the 1950s. It was her internal spaces that created the biggest impression. Here was up-to-the-

FAIRSEA

***Fairsea* in varying stages of her reconstruction at Trieste.** *Arthur Crook.*

An artist's impression, rather elongated, of the elegant 'new' Sitmar liners, *Fairsea* and *Fairwind*.
Author's collection.

minute Italian design at sea. Bold and dramatic colours were used everywhere, with strikingly sculptured furnishings, textured metallic walls, gleaming bone white linoleum and wall-sized murals. It was a world away from those traditional Cunard interiors and *Aquitania*'s dining chairs. The ship had been stripped of every last trace of Cunard-style décor; and, while the basic structure and layout of some of the public rooms remained, along with some of the staircases and lift shafts, there was nothing to give even the faintest hint of her previous life. *Fairsea* was to all intents a new ship.

Every one of her cabins had been rebuilt and now all of them had their own private bathrooms and had been reconstructed to give passengers much more space. The ship now had the facility to carry 884 passengers in mainly double-occupancy cabins, just 16 more than in her days as *Carinthia* when many had travelled in four-berth cabins. By creating cabins in the extended superstructure, in some former crew areas and in the now redundant cargo holds, Sitmar's designers had given her 236 outside and 232 inside cabins. All were much more spacious than in the days when, as *Carinthia*, she had 160 outside and 188 inside.

Almost all the decks had been renamed. Only Promenade Deck retained its old title. What had been Sports, Boat, Promenade, Main, 'A', Restaurant and 'B' decks were now Europa, Ocean, Promenade, Monte Carlo, Acapulco, Riviera, Bahamas, Continental and 'D'. *Fairsea* now boasted an increased number of public rooms, with a large forward-facing nightclub on Ocean Deck. The Main Lounge was now forward on Promenade Deck, in the location of the old First Class Smoking Room, the First Class open promenade and number three cargo hatchway. Aft, there was an extensive array of shops, and another lounge where the cinema had been. There was now a library and cocktail bar and where the Tourist Class Lounge had once been was now an alternative dining room, called The Grill Room, together with a small casino and a writing room. What had once been open deck was now known as the South Pacific Lounge. Both the existing dining rooms were retained: the former Tourist Class Restaurant, while totally transformed in decorative style, was otherwise unchanged, neither enlarged nor altered structurally in any way. The rather smaller First Class Restaurant, on the other hand, was considerably enlarged by the inclusion of space that had been crew accommodation and the hospital (which had been relocated elsewhere). In every way, the ship had been transformed from an enclosed liner built for a 5-day North Atlantic crossing into an elegant and modern cruise ship suited to long-haul voyages. It seemed very appropriate that in early publicity material heralding the entry of *Fairwind* and *Fairsea* into service, Sitmar should say that "The era of the great cruise ship has not entirely disappeared".

The completely transformed *Fairsea* left Trieste on the 3rd November, 1971 for Los Angeles, calling at Cadiz, St. Thomas, Antigua and Acapulco en route. The voyage was a series of several firsts for the former Cunarder: her first time through the Panama Canal, the first time she had ventured into the Pacific and her first calls in both Mexico and California – places that would all become very familiar to her in the following years. Having arrived at Los Angeles on the 9th December, she then continued up to San Francisco, where she was officially presented to the press and representatives of the travel industry.

On the 14th December, *Fairsea* began her cruise service down to Mexico. This first cruise turned out to be memorable in more ways than one, particularly for some crew members. Sixty-nine stewards and five stewardesses went on strike regarding an overtime issue. The Captain refused to concede to their demands and ordered the ship to sail, leaving the strikers ashore without passports or money and in just the clothes they were wearing. Aboard *Fairsea*, deck crew took their places as public room and cabin stewards, while ashore, the US authorities took pity on the stranded crewmembers. Visas were issued to them so that they were able to return home. It was unfortunate that the issue should end up in the courts. After several months the former crew had their belongings returned to them and Sitmar paid them all that was owing to them. It was an unhappy beginning to their new cruise venture.

The transformation was total. The new interiors were sleekly modern. *Author's collection.*

The cruises were of six days: southbound, the ship would depart Los Angeles at 8 pm and after two days at sea would arrive in Puerto Vallarta. The following day was also spent at sea before arriving in Acapulco on the morning of the sixth day. The passengers would use the ship as their hotel that day and it was not until the

The Lido Bar had an entire wall of glass looking out over one of the pools. *Arthur Crook.*

following day that they would transfer to hotels in the city, flying home three days later. For the northbound cruise, passengers would fly down to Acapulco and after three nights there would board *Fairsea* for the cruise home via Zihuatanejo and Mazatlan. Both the southbound and the northbound cruises could be combined to make a twelve day round trip.

The conversion of *Fairwind* had progressed at a much slower rate than that of her sister and it was not until June, 1972 that she was completed. Again, the work had been extensive, stripping her back to the original structure before effecting another remarkable transformation. She sailed from Trieste on the 14th June, 1972, virtually a replica of *Fairsea*. Only some aspects of internal décor set the two ships apart. As had been the case with her sister, Umberto Nordio had been responsible for *Fairwind*'s interiors. He had already been involved in the interior design of many famous Italian liners and it was perhaps fitting that *Fairsea* and *Fairwind*, which attracted so much interest, should be his final ships. Unfortunately, he died shortly before they entered Sitmar's service.

As well as the extensive safety features that had been incorporated during the conversions, both vessels had been fitted with biological sewage treatment plants, the first ships to have them. Having been so extensive, the conversions caused considerable interest within the shipbuilding industry and particularly with both Lloyd's Register and the United States Coast Guard. Lloyd's Register featured the conversions of both ships in their publication 100 A1 and, of course, the USCG paid the ships special attention once they arrived in US waters. Glowing with pride, Sitmar called them 'the most luxurious ever seen in most parts of the world'. They also went on to state that the line had 'gone to a great deal of trouble to ensure that the ships are not only abreast of the times but a few years ahead'.

The initial voyage of *Fairwind* out to Los Angeles was even more extensive than that of her sister. She made calls at Cadiz and Port Everglades. There her official 'maiden voyage' began when she left on the 3rd July, 1972 for St. Thomas, La Guaira and St. Anna Bay, then through the Panama Canal and up to Acapulco and, finally, Los Angeles. She departed on her first Mexican Riviera cruise on the 14th August.

Between August and November, *Fairsea* was employed on two rather longer cruise itineraries: seventeen days from Los Angeles to Acapulco, Balboa, through the Panama Canal, Cristobal, Cartagena, Aruba, Martinique, San Juan and Port Everglades. After an overnight stop at the Florida port, she would begin the return cruise to Los Angeles. This was also of 17 days and, by calling at different Caribbean ports, enabled the round trip to be marketed as a 35-day cruise.

However, passenger loads were very low. This was despite the ships' luxurious modernity, the fact that they were considerably larger than any others employed on cruises to Mexico at that time and that they offered the then unique service of single-sitting dining as well as the alternative dining option of The Grill Room. There, 'specialities are cooked to order as you watch'. These were options that are now taken for granted by most cruise passengers but were then a great novelty. On occasions, the ships would sail with only a hundred or so passengers aboard. Several factors seemed to blame, particularly Sitmar's lack of experience in the cruise market, as well as their unpreparedness for dealing with the expectations of American passengers. The company learned the hard way that an all-year-round luxury cruise operation was very different from sending what was essentially a migrant class vessel on a fun cruise over Christmas.

It did not help that Sitmar tried to sell their cruises direct, rather than through travel agents. Given that they were almost unknown in the United States, this was a recipe for disaster. Fortunately, Sitmar executives realised quickly that their marketing strategy was not working and that their investment in the ships was vanishing. It was essential to get the travel agents on their side. The direct sell operation was dropped and the cruises were now marketed in the regular way, through the agents. With the promotion that the travel industry was able to give to the ships, business slowly began to pick up. The Italian food and service were emphasised, as was the fact that *Fairsea* and *Fairwind* were more luxurious than any others in Pacific cruising at that time. The fact that, built to cope with the worst the North Atlantic could throw at them, they were very stable and sea-kindly also helped to enhance their reputation.

***Sylvania*, dressed overall, at New York.** *Donald Stoltenberg.*

The distinctive Mounties' Bar on the *Ivernia*. *Captain Ron Warwick collection.*

Disporting themselves in the sunshine, *Carmania*'s passengers enjoy her stylish Lido Deck.
Captain Ron Warwick.

***Franconia*'s impressive bow towers above Front Street, Hamilton, Bermuda.** *Captain Ron Warwick.*

A stern view of *Franconia* at Piraeus, showing off the Lido she acquired during her conversion. *Arthur Crook.*

***Fairwind* and *Fairland* laid up at Southampton, awaiting the finalisation of plans for their conversion.** *Donald Stoltenberg.*

***Fairwind* nearing completion at Trieste in March, 1972.** *Arthur Crook.*

***Fairsea* departing Los Angeles in August, 1984.** *Peter Knego.*

This aerial view of *Fairwind*'s Lido, with its three pools, emphasises the transformation of an Atlantic liner into a cruise ship. *Alberto Bisagno collection.*

The renamed *Sitmar Fairwind* shows off her new livery at Port Everglades on the 3rd August 1988.
Victor Scrivens photograph. Timothy J. Dacey collection.

Nearing the end of her career but still looking immaculate, *Fedor Shalyapin* at Lisbon. *Luis Miguel Correia.*

Dignified in decay, *Leonid Sobinov* and *Fedor Shalyapin* laid up at Ilichevsk. *Peter Knego.*

Dawn Princess **alongside at Lisbon in May, 1989 at the beginning of her career with Princess Cruises.** *Luís Miguel Correia.*

The distinctively Italian funnel of *Fair Princess*. *Peter Knego.*

***Albatros*, newly repaired after her May, 1997 Scilly Isles grounding, alongside at Southampton.** *Mark Cornford.*

Cruising in the South Seas, *Fair Princess* in P&O livery. *Clive Harvey.*

From Red Duster To Red Flag

While *Fairsea* and *Fairwind* were beginning to prove themselves in the luxury cruise market, their former fleetmates, *Carmania* and *Franconia*, were still swinging idly at their lay-up moorings in the River Fal, awaiting a buyer and meanwhile causing concern to the accountants at Cunard. For a time, it had seemed that their salvation would come from shipping entrepreneur Ted Arison of the fledgling Carnival Cruise Lines. In 1971, he had gone to London to negotiate with Cunard for the acquisition of the laid-up liners. Unable to agree terms, he turned his attention elsewhere and *Carmania* and *Franconia* remained idle for many more months.

Then, in August, 1973, it was announced that they had been sold to Panamanian interests, Nikreis Maritime Corporation. It seemed a very complicated transaction as it was also announced at the time that Nikreis Maritime were affiliated to a New York-based company known as Robin International. For a while, it was not apparent what the future held for the liners. Nothing about the sale seemed to be straightforward and there was a great deal of non-cooperation from the parties involved. Although it was eventually revealed that the ships would, in fact, fly the 'Hammer And Sickle' of the Soviet Union as units of their then mighty passenger fleet, it was believed at the time that they were actually owned by Nikreis and merely bareboat chartered to the Russians.

When it was reported that the former *Franconia* would sail as the *Fedor Shalyapin*, Lloyd's List commented: "This news raises many questions about the status of the *Carmania* and *Franconia*.... Very few answers have been forthcoming. As far as can be ascertained, the *Fedor Shalyapin* will operate under the Russian flag and carry a Russian crew. Nikreis Maritime Corporation, the purchasers, are affiliated to the New York-based Robin International Corporation, an import-export company which, it is believed, has close business ties with Russia, either directly or indirectly." Apparently, no approach to buy the ships was made by the Russians, either to Cunard

Now under the Hammer and Sickle, the former *Franconia* and *Carmania* are being refitted in Newcastle. *Arthur Crook.*

***Leonid Sobinov* operated moderately-priced cruises out of Southampton for CTC Lines.** *Author's collection.*

or to the shipbrokers who handled the sale. All dealings had been through Nikreis Maritime and it would seem that the managers of Morpasflot (Seagoing Passenger Fleet) had little, if any, knowledge of the ships until they were offered to them either by Nikreis or Robin International. It is unlikely that the sale of two such prominent passenger liners had ever before been the subject of such subterfuge. Thus, all four Saxonia sisters now found themselves in Russian hands. While the former *Carmania* and *Franconia* were about to hoist the Red Flag of Soviet Russia, the one-time *Carinthia* and *Sylvania* were now owned by the Vlasov family of White Russian, Cossack origin.

Before entering service for their new owners, it was arranged for the *Carmania* and *Franconia* to be overhauled by Swan, Hunter on the Tyne. The *Franconia* was the first to leave the River Fal, sailing from there on the 14th August, 1973; she was followed by *Carmania* on the 30th August. They arrived on the Tyne on the 17th August and 1st September, respectively. Between the announcement of her sale and her departure from the lay-up berth, it had been announced that *Carmania* would adopt the name *Leonid Sobinov*.

Quite coincidentally, Australia would feature significantly in the future of both ships, just as it had at one time seemed it would for their two younger sisters. The Soviet Union, in great need of hard currency, was willing to underwrite the operational costs of liners such as the former Cunarders. There was thus no need for them to court the Australian government for what the western-based shipping lines saw as the essential migrant-carrying contract. So, instead of the former *Carinthia* and *Sylvania* making line voyages out to Australia with budget-minded tourists and migrants in search of new lives, the role fell instead to the former *Carmania* and *Franconia*, now called *Leonid Sobinov* and *Fedor Shalyapin*. These were names which recalled famous Russian opera singers of the early years of the century.

The overhaul work on *Fedor Shalyapin* was completed first and on the 20th November, 1973, she sailed from Southampton for Australia under the banner of CTC Lines. It was not until February, 1974 that *Leonid Sobinov* joined her. Little had been done to change them internally. The layout and décor of their public rooms and cabins remained exactly as it had been when the ships

An extensive cruise programme was also operated out of Sydney under the CTC banner. *Author's collection.*

The ambience of a Soviet liner was a far cry from that of a Cunarder. *Author's collection.*

had sailed for Cunard. Even the coathangers in the wardrobes were still stamped 'Cunard Line'. The only apparent alteration was to the names of the public rooms. The work had centred mainly on the ships' machinery, ensuring that the long months of inactivity had not created any problems. The most obvious external change was that now the funnels were painted white with a broad red band that carried the golden crossed Hammer and Sickle emblem. On both bow and stern the names were spelled out in Cyrillic lettering. The ships were registered in Odessa and came under the ownership of the Black Sea Shipping Company.

Once they reached Australia, both *Leonid Sobinov* and *Fedor Shalyapin* embarked on a programme of cruises out of Sydney. The *Sobinov* was, however, soon heading back to Europe while the *Shalyapin* remained in Far Eastern and Pacific waters. By June, she was scheduled to be in Yokohama and CTC Lines were offering the opportunity for British tourists to fly to Japan via Moscow (where they would spend two nights) and then to join the ship. She was described as "tss *Fedor Shalyapin*, 21,500 tons of ocean-going luxury." She sailed to a variety of fascinating ports before arriving in Fremantle and then Sydney. Prices for this remarkable trip were low, even for 1974: from £239 to Fremantle and £259 to Sydney.

It would appear that there were no clauses in the contract of the sale of the former *Carmania* and *Franconia* restricting their areas of operation, as had been the case with *Carinthia* and *Sylvania*. By July, once *Leonid Sobinov* was again in the more familiar European and based on Southampton, she operated a series of five cruises, going to the North Cape and into the Mediterranean as far as Alexandria, areas familiar to the four sisters during their final Cunard years. Perhaps, given their great desire to dispose of the ships, Cunard did not want to inhibit any potential sale by insisting on restrictive clauses in the contract.

CTC Lines went to considerable lengths to introduce *Leonid Sobinov* to the UK market. The Russian cruise fleet seemed likely at that time simply to continue expanding. CTC Lines even issued a mock newspaper, Cruise News – CTC Lines, to promote the company and the ships they had the responsibility for marketing. The acquisition of the luxurious former German cruise ship *Hamburg* and of the ex-Cunarders gave Cruise News great copy and they did not hesitate to mention that ".... *Leonid Sobinov* was until last year none other than the famous Cunard Line's *Carmania.* Since then she has been refurbished to our own very high standards and is now a one class ship." Given the fares that CTC were charging, one could hardly have expected her passengers to complain.

In fact, it was quite obvious when one stepped aboard that little had been done to spruce up what had once been those striking interiors. They were quite tired and dated in places and it was obvious why Cunard had felt the need to retire the ships. Serious investment would have been required to update them. However, the *Leonid Sobinov* was something of a time-warp, as most of the public rooms retained the same furnishings and décor they had when she first re-emerged from John Brown's as *Carmania.* It seemed as though CTC Lines were trading on that heritage and the ship's former reputation for all they were worth. In some respects, it apparently worked – though it fell somewhat flat once one stepped into the dining room. The Russians' idea of cruise ship cuisine was considerably different from that of Cunard Line. Nevertheless, *Leonid Sobinov* appears to have acquired a degree of popularity during her first season of Southampton-based cruises.

Her final cruise of that 1974 season ended in Malta on

Russian-style entertainment was a feature of Soviet cruise ships. *Author's collection.*

Plus ça change, plus c'est la même chose. The Soviet *Fedor Shalyapin* in 1981 and (below) under Ukrainian ownership in 1994. *Clive Harvey and John Adams.*

the 9th September and the following month she was again making her way out to Australia and New Zealand, this time via the Cape route. However, at that time Russian ships were not allowed to put in at South African ports, so having called at Las Palmas, Dakar and St. Helena, she then rounded the Cape of Good Hope without a call and her next stop was Mauritius. *Leonid Sobinov* then made her way up to Singapore before arriving at Fremantle, Melbourne, Sydney and Auckland.

This was to be the pattern of her service for several years, with most of her cruises being operated out of Australia. Her schedule of Pacific cruises sometimes ran from mid-December through to early May, while her European cruise programme was rather shorter. In 1976, for example, it was barely two months – from the 20th June to the 26th August – but included the classic itineraries to the Baltic capitals, the Canary Islands and the western Mediterranean.

Leonid Sobinov spent the greater part of 1979 on the regular line service between Sydney and Southampton. She had left Sydney for Europe on the 15th January and had arrived in Southampton on the 20th February. The following day, she began another long voyage down to Australia, arriving there at the end of March. After a little more than a month cruising out of Sydney, she was heading back to Southampton, arriving there on the 18th June. At 11 pm that same night, she departed on a cruise to the Mediterranean and the Black Sea. This ended at Odessa and her passengers were returned home by air. It would appear that this was her final cruise from Southampton, the port that, as a Cunarder, she had once called home. She was, however, back there on the 16th November, preparing for another line voyage to Australia, which she reached just in time for Christmas. The CTC liner service to the Antipodes appeared to be thriving, the voyages of *Leonid Sobinov* being just part of a bigger schedule with the liners *Taras Shevchenko, Ivan Franko* and *Mikhail Lermontov* also thus employed. In 1980, however, *Leonid Sobinov* made only two such voyages, the first departing Sydney on the 14th May, arriving at Southampton a month later; then towards the end of the year, on the 18th November, she left Southampton for Australia. After that, her visits to England were rather less frequent.

While *Leonid Sobinov* divided her time between Europe and Australia, *Fedor Shalyapin* had been employed principally out of Australia and in the Orient. Between May and November, 1976, she undertook a series of Pacific cruises under charter to Shaw Savill Cruises of Australia. It was during this charter that a much-reported and yet never verified incident took place. *Fedor Shalyapin* was crossing the Tasman Sea on her way from Auckland to Sydney when, in the early hours of the morning, the ship suddenly stopped and all her lights were extinguished. Those passengers still partying, about 200 in all, heard the ship's cranes start up and saw a submarine come alongside. There was then a transfer of both goods and personnel between the two vessels. The incident was, of course, denied by the officials at the Embassy of the Soviet Union and Shaw Savill said they knew nothing about it. This curious encounter will, it seems, remain a mystery.

Once in a while, one of her voyages would be marketed in Europe. Such was the case in 1979 when she ran an 18-day cruise from Singapore to Sydney via Jakarta, Surabaya, Bali, Fremantle and Melbourne. A similar voyage, but departing Hong Kong, was offered for December, obviously aimed at Australians who wanted to get home in time for the Christmas holidays. These were marketed through a company specialising in 'Fly/Ship' voyages between Europe and Australia, with passengers being flown out to a Far East port and completing their journey by sea. Various vessels were used, including Singapore-owned ships as well as another Russian, the 5,000-ton *Turkmenia*. It turned out to be a rather significant December, as it was then that Soviet troops invaded Afghanistan. As a consequence, the Australian government banned all Russian passenger ships from their ports. The ban took effect from February, 1980. *Leonid Sobinov* was the first to leave and *Fedor Shalyapin* followed very soon after, both heading for Vladivostock.

Without this lucrative charter work, the two former Cunarders were now used on the most diverse routes – to places of political unrest such as Angola, for example, where there was some Soviet involvement. They carried passengers euphemistically referred to as 'technicians'. On other occasions, they were to be found on voyages from the Black Sea, across the Atlantic to Cuba, with a mixed load of Soviet tourists, troops and, again, those 'technicians'.

Apart from such dubious employment, both *Leonid Sobinov* and *Fedor Shalyapin* were chartered out to tour companies. By 1981, *Fedor Shalyapin* was back in northern Europe and in the Spring made at least two calls in London. It was announced that in 1982 she would make a 97-night Round the World cruise calling at 21 ports. Not even at the height of her career with Cunard had she undertaken such a fabulous journey and the itinerary was as imaginative as it was lengthy. There were to be calls at such diverse ports as Guayaquil, Lima and Pitcairn Island, a two day stay at Yokohama, calls at Bangkok and the rarely visited Maldive Islands and then up through the more familiar ports of the Mediterranean – all that for as little as £1,839 (in a 4-berth inside cabin on B Deck) or for the princely sum of £7,599 for a Main Deck de luxe cabin. Sadly, it was not to be. Instead, the very recently refurbished and rather newer *Mikhail Lermontov*, at that time the 'prestige ship' of the CTC Lines operation, undertook the cruise.

Fedor Shalyapin was chartered by the German tour company Jahn Reisen GmbH for several years in the early/mid-1980s and it seemed that this would be her final burst of glory. During the summer months she made 10- and 14-day cruises out of Genoa to ports round the Mediterranean. In the winters, she was cruising in what were now her most familiar waters, those of the Far East. However, with the introduction of the Belorussiya class of ferry/cruise ships, *Leonid Sobinov* and *Fedor Shalyapin* were seen less and less in Europe. The new, purpose-built ships seemed to take their places not only on the cruise itineraries but, quite remarkably, also on the long-haul voyages to Australia and, on occasions, around the World. On the 20th June, 1986, *Fedor Shalyapin* was involved in an unfortunate accident when she collided with the tug *Amadores II* while at Piraeus. The tug sank, with the loss of one crewmember.

On the 31st August, 1986 came the horrific news that the veteran, 61-year old Soviet liner *Admiral Nachimov* had sunk as a result of a collision during a Black Sea voyage. The elderly liner went down rapidly and with considerable loss of life. In 'shock horror' style, the World's media reported the age not only of the sunken vessel but also of many others in the huge and diverse Soviet passenger fleet. As a result, radical changes were announced: all ships built before 1960 would be disposed of and replaced with new and modern vessels which would be suited to the newly reforming Soviet Union. It seemed then that the end was in sight for the former Cunarders, that they would be swept away, along with other handsome yet dated vessels, victims of Mikhail Gorbachov's reforming zeal. The collapse of the Soviet system in 1989 rather suddenly brought to an end to such radical plans. There were other, far higher priorities to be dealt with. The countries which had once been combined as the Soviet Union became independent states. These monumental changes naturally affected what had once been the huge, centrally-controlled Soviet merchant shipping fleet.

At first, as a result, the two ships became part of the Ukrainian fleet. Then, in 1990, *Leonid Sobinov* was registered under the ownership of Transblasco Four Shipping Co.Ltd. of Valletta, Malta, but was managed by Transorient Overseas SA, also of Valletta. In 1992, *Fedor Shalyapin* was registered under the ownership of Odessa Cruise (Fedor Shalyapin) Co., another Valletta-registered concern. The real ownership of the vessels still lay in the Ukraine, however. (Although both ships had been registered in Odessa as part of the Black Sea Shipping Company fleet, at some point *Fedor Shalyapin* was listed as being owned by the Far Eastern Shipping Company. However, when she called at Tilbury in 1981, Odessa was clearly her port of registry.)

Now, with greater freedom being afforded to former citizens of the Soviet Union to travel abroad, it seemed as though the two ships might have acquired a new lease of life as they were often seen in the Mediterranean ports on cruises from the Black Sea. Gone now was the red band and the Hammer and Sickle on the funnel. Instead, *Fedor Shalyapin* had a broad blue band with a white and gold logo of a bird in flight. *Leonid Sobinov*'s funnel, on the other hand, carried an abstract design of three blue lines over a distorted red triangle. It was a world away from the formality of the impressive Cunard red and black.

For a while, both ships continued to sail, looking pristine and well-maintained. In 1989, *Leonid Sobinov* underwent mechanical repairs and refitting work at Piraeus. Unfortunately, many of her better furnishings were replaced with cheaper fittings. However, it was becoming increasingly obvious to their Ukrainian owners that the ships were too expensive to run and maintain, especially without the benefit of the state-supported Morpasflot to underwrite the costs. In the mid-summer of 1994, *Fedor Shalyapin* made an extended cruise from St.Petersburg, calling at twenty ports around Europe and in the Mediterranean, ending at Odessa. To the casual observer, she still looked magnificent, if somewhat dated. Her paintwork was pristine and she had a smart blue band around her hull. But on closer inspection, her foredeck could be seen to be loaded with cars, apparently bought second-hand in Germany by passengers who intended to resell them once they returned home. On the quayside, when the ship tied up in Lisbon or Naples, crew members sold tools, military memorabilia, anything they could lay their hands on in a desperate attempt to make money. Visitors were not allowed aboard. The air-conditioning had failed and the crew, less concerned about security, were embarrassed to let Westerners see the folorn state of the ship's interior. The end was clearly in sight. The first two of the Saxonia sisters had barely a year left to sail in these reduced circumstances. By the autumn of 1995, both *Leonid Sobinov* and *Fedor Shalyapin* were placed in lay-up at Ilichevsk, a Black Sea port some forty kilometres south-west of Odessa.

The American ship historian Peter Knego managed to engineer a visit to the laid-up liners in July, 1997 and from his report it was obvious that, after just those eighteen months of inactivity, coupled with their already run-down state, they would never sail commercially again. Peter remembered his visit to the ships in vivid detail:

"Finally, the black-domed funnels of the *Leonid Sobinov* and *Fedor Shalyapin* appeared through a forest of cranes and dockside buildings. Both ships had their bows pointing out into the bay, extending far beyond their respective piers. *Fedor Shalyapin* awaited us at the end of her slip, her white hull bearing faint streaks of rust. She was listing slightly to starboard. We met some of the ship's attending crew at the gangway, which led into the foyer aft on Restaurant Deck. In pitch darkness, we climbed three decks to the dual level lounge on Promenade Deck. The one notable architectural difference between *Fedor Shalyapin* and *Leonid Sobinov* can be found in the aft staircase linking the two levels of the lounge. On the former, it sweeps in a graceful arc down from the starboard Boat Deck balcony, while on the latter it begins with small flights on either side that converge in the middle, flaring out slightly toward the lower level.

"We proceeded along the portside enclosed promenade, at one time *Fedor Shalyapin*'s popular Winter Garden. While the handsome wooden furnishings remained, the plants had long since died and remains of their dried brown tendrils still clung to bamboo trellises. I peered in through the windows to the former First Class bar/lounge, but this elegant room was locked. Sadly, nearly all of the public rooms were locked up and in the

***Fedor Shalyapin* in July, 1994, sailing from the Thames for the last time. Note the second-hand cars on her deck, ready for resale when their owners reach home.** *Clive Harvey.*

case of the Promenade Deck spaces their curtains were drawn, thus preventing me from even taking photographs through the windows.

"Following the crew, I worked my way up a pitch-dark staircase to Bridge Deck. The thick wooden banisters were similar to some found aboard the *Queen Mary*. The chart room was on the port side and led to the wheelhouse just forward. It was a magnificent space, its vintage equipment dominated by a large polished brass wheel and framed in a backdrop of rich wood panelling, pale grey fixtures and the large windows. The upper decks were painted pale blue and were showing their lack of maintenance. In many places, the paint was cracked or marred by rust.

"We went down to the aft Sports Deck. Protected by screens to either side, it overlooked the gracefully curved lido area with its pair of semi-spiral staircases and, unfortunately, stained green astro-turf. I worked my way through the midships games areas, past the towering, domed funnel. Up forward, I found the glass-enclosed Sun Room, once the First Class solarium but now a lonely space with worn brown carpeting and tattered curtains. The exterior decking on this part of the ship was covered with water-soaked blue astro-turf and on close inspection the outlines of the wooden planks underneath showed through. The group waited for me as I went to the fo'c'stle to take some shots of the forward superstructure and the builder's plate. The forward Promenade Deck observation area was filled with rusting scrap and water from the recent rains. When I returned, we proceeded down the aft staircase, which at Promenade Deck level boasted a large portrait of *Fedor Shalyapin*, the renowned opera singer. In pitch blackness, we stopped at the Purser's office on A Deck and then disembarked via the gangway aft on Restaurant Deck.

"Off to the port side, *Leonid Sobinov*, her comrade in decay, awaited us and two friendly crew members welcomed us at the gangway. I began my photography in the cavernous aft dining room, which they kindly lit with emergency generators. The spartan space had brown flooring, bare wooden tables and plain white bulkheads which had back-lit panels in lieu of portholes. The galley, just forward, was reached via an ornate iron gate, which was locked.

"Our hosts led us back through the aft lobby and up to the Promenade Deck where we proceeded forward along the starboard side. Unlike her sister's, this Promenade Deck did not sport a Winter Garden and was quite clean. Even though the forward bar/lounge was locked, a window on the starboard side was open, allowing me to photograph the full length of the room. The bar was in the far corner, its shiny brass façade behind rows of stacked furniture. Our friends unlocked the doors to the midships

***Fedor Shalyapin* (foreground) and *Leonid Sobinov* lying at Ilichevsk, awaiting their fate.** *Peter Knego.*

lounge… the elegant space had a raised dome in its central ceiling, which sported two spindly chandeliers (those were the specially-designed light fittings made for the room when the ship was transformed into the *Carmania*). A bar was forward and faced the wooden dance floor and orchestra stand. The dance floor was filled with large potted plants that had long since expired, leaving a residue of dirt and leaves along its length. We then moved into the dual-level lounge, the lower portion of which had been stripped of its furnishings. Vivid maroon carpeting and stark white walls made the room seem larger than its counterpart on the *Fedor Shalyapin*.

"I worked my way to the aft promenade lobby, where the stairwell, unlike that aboard the sister vessel, did not contain a portrait of the ship's namesake – *Leonid Sobinov*, another great Russian opera singer/actor. (One can only assume that it had been removed as it had hung there in the days when the liner was sailing from Southampton.) The ceiling was vintage Cunard, with rectangular plaster light fittings suspended from arched recesses. With flashlights, we found our way into the midships cinema balcony, its unspoilt condition revealed only by the camera's flash. We examined a couple of de luxe cabins on the starboard side Main Deck. The fittings were steel and bakelite and similar to some of those on the *Queen Mary*. A visit to the wheelhouse followed, another study in well-maintained vintage British navigation equipment.

"The next morning, we drove back to Ilichevsk to finish documenting the *Leonid Sobinov*. Before driving to the shipyard, we stopped at a vantage point across the bay and for $50 a tug was arranged to take us alongside the vessels for optimal footage. The tug was, rather ironically, called *Albatros*, the name currently shared by the former *Sylvania*. Our captain was most accommodating, patiently stopping and starting his vessel as we clamoured for the best angles.

"Our visit resumed with a look at an A Deck cabin, number 102. Our host, the ship's former Chief Engineer, pointed out all its original fixtures, proudly exclaiming "Carmania! English!" with each discovery. He pulled aside a weathered wooden and leather footstool with *Carmania* stamped on its underside and presented it

A vintage scene on the bridge of *Fedor Shalyapin*, giving the illusion that the ship was ready to sail. *Peter Knego.*

to us. This was accompanied by an old Australian newspaper clipping showing the *Leonid Sobinov* entering Sydney Heads in a terrific gale, and some rolled cloth builders' plans of the *Saxonia*. I was overwhelmed by his kindness and obvious pride in the beautiful old ship's heritage. The after decks of *Leonid Sobinov* were not covered with astro-turf like the *Fedor Shalyapin*'s. The teak planks were stained by rust and needed work but were otherwise intact. The Sports Deck was the same as the *Fedor Shalyapin*'s, except that it was covered in a layer of thick green paint instead of astro-turf. After a final visit to the purser's office, we reluctantly returned to the aft Restaurant Deck lobby to bid farewell to our hosts and the once proud Cunarder. Our final view of the two graceful dowager liners was from the highway as we drove back to Odessa.

In stark contrast to the décor of her Cunard days, *Fedor Shalyapin*'s Main Lounge now presented a depressing sight. *Peter Knego*.

"The future holds little hope for either ship. The *Fedor Shalyapin* reportedly needs some $16 million in mechanical repairs and, while it appears otherwise, we were told that her facilities are in better operating condition than those of the *Leonid Sobinov*. The *Sobinov* is said to be mechanically sound but has nonetheless been readied for the tow to an overseas scrapyard. Despite this, her owners were soliciting for a last minute charter to keep her trading."

There was, of course, no hope of any last minute charter. Apart from the worn condition of both liners, stringent new Safety Of Life At Sea regulations were due to be enforced just two months after Peter's visit – regulations which, even if the ships had still been sailing, would have required either their withdrawal or an investment of several million pounds to bring them up to compliance. By the following spring, it was rumoured that *Leonid Sobinov* had gone to Indian ship breakers but the story, though widely reported, proved to be incorrect. The proud old liners remained at their lay-up berths in Ilichevsk, awaiting their fate. It actually seemed that someone thought there might be life in at least one of the pair. Enquiries were received from a company who wanted to operate *Fedor Shalyapin* on a run between India and the United Arab Emirates for the transport of Indian workers. However, the project never materialised. Cheap air fares and limited vacation time for the workers made it an uneconomic proposition.

Then, on the 27th January, 1999, *Leonid Sobinov* sailed for Odessa. She arrived there the same day and preparations were made for her final voyage. The now shabby liner left Odessa on the 30th January and passed through the Suez Canal on the 10th February. Although her destination was not reported, it was, as rumoured, the breaker's yards of India. But, although still proudly under her own steam rather than under tow, the old former Cunarder gave a final show of reluctance to face her impending demise – she ran out of fuel and went adrift in the Indian Ocean. However, she was retrieved by tugs and was eventually anchored off Alang on the 1st April. At that point, negotiations were underway possibly to use her as an accommodation ship but in the end it was decided that as her condition was so poor the plan to scrap her should go ahead. After sitting at anchor under the blistering Indian sun, she was dragged ashore for breaking, by the tugs *Lion King* and *Neftegaz 52*, on the 1st October, 1999. Even then, it seemed as though she was exerting some control over her demise, for on the 8th May, 2000 there was a strike by the workers in the ship breaking yard, affecting the dismantling process.

Thus ended the career of the former *Saxonia*, one of the most significant, if not entirely successful, British liners of the 1950s. Nevertheless, it was a tribute to her builders that she had survived for almost 45 years. It cannot possibly have been imagined as she slid down those launch ways at John Brown's, the winter sunshine illuminating the emblem of the rampant Cunard lion on her stem, that she would in fact find greater success on the long-haul liner route to Australia under the red flag of Soviet Russia than she did on the Atlantic under the Red Duster of the United Kingdom.

At the time of writing, her sister *Fedor Shalyapin* is left to decay in lonely lay-up at Ilichevsk.

***Leonid Sobinov*, being readied for her final voyage, is seen from the snow-covered deck of her sister.**
Peter Knego.

The Glory Days of Sitmar

Very soon after the introduction into service of *Fairsea* and *Fairwind*, Sitmar Line changed the emphasis of their operations. Having run long-haul trans-oceanic voyages with some cruises, they now became almost exclusively a cruise line. By 1971, they felt there were insufficient numbers of passengers to justify using their two liners *Fairsky* and *Fairstar* on the service between Britain and Australia. They therefore withdrew *Fairsky* and in February, 1972 she was placed in lay-up in Southampton. She remained there until November, 1973 when she was re-activated for three trips to Australia before being placed in permanent cruise service out of Australian ports.

Her fleetmate, *Fairstar*, was by this time making fewer line voyages and more Sydney-based cruises. Although these were very successful, the line decided that, with *Fairsky* also cruising out of Australia and with *Fairsea* and *Fairwind* beginning to make an impression on the American market, they would experiment with *Fairstar* in the British cruise market. A whole programme of cruises was scheduled for her, sailing out of Southampton, during the summer of 1974. Sadly, they were not a resounding success. The very traditional British cruise market was at that time well served by liners whose owners understood their passengers' tastes: P&O's mighty *Canberra* and *Oriana* which, for at least part of that summer, were accompanied by the *Himalaya* in her final months of service; and, for a brief while longer, Shaw Savill's beautiful *Northern Star* and her fleet-mate *Ocean Monarch*. There was considerable loyalty to these ships that were well-established in the UK cruising scene. They were to some extent supported by the likes of the Chandris Lines vessels and the Russian ships under charter to CTC Lines. They were more than enough to cope with the British cruise market. It is also possible that, in the UK, Sitmar was looked upon as an emigrant-carrier and therefore *Fairstar* was regarded as an emigrant ship. At the end of the failed experiment, Sitmar returned *Fairstar* to Australia where she was already popular. Over the years, that popularity as a cruise ship grew to an almost legendary status.

A rare meeting of *Fairsea* and *Fairwind* off St. Croix in the U.S. Virgin Islands. *Alberto Bisagno*

By 1975, Sitmar ceased all liner operations, severing their links with those long voyages between Britain and Australia. The name Sitmar Line ceased to exist. From then onward the company was known as Sitmar Cruises and concentrated purely on the Australian and American cruise markets. The next few years were to see radical changes in ocean liner transportation to Australia. Not only did Sitmar decide to withdraw but there was also the premature departure for the breakers' yards of both the Shaw Savill liners, *Northern Star* and *Ocean Monarch.* It was, however, just at the time these companies ceased their Britain to Australia services that the Russians introduced the former *Carmania* onto the route as the *Leonid Sobinov*. Indeed, there were still a few other liners sailing on the route. Chandris, of course, still had the Australian government contract. P&O continued to maintain a presence on what was a very traditional service for them, albeit on a rather more seasonal basis since most of their famous liners that had served on the route during the previous two decades had gone to the breakers by the mid-1970s. Then there were still the Italians, with the magnificent *Galileo Galilei* and *Guglielmo Marconi* of Lloyd Triestino sailing out of Genoa.

Time, however, was running out for all these liners. The splendid *Australis* of Chandris Lines departed Southampton on her final voyage to Australia in November, 1977. In future government-sponsored migrants would be transported by air. The year 1977 also saw the withdrawal from the Australian service of *Galileo Galilei*, while in the previous year her sister *Guglielmo Marconi* had been transferred to Italia for their South American service. Most ironically of all, *Leonid Sobinov* and *Fedor Shalyapin*, which had appeared on the scene at seemingly just the right time, to operate a service for those who would never wish to fly or who preferred a leisurely way of travel, were banned from Australian ports because of Russia's invasion of Afghanistan.

It had perhaps been a wise decision by Sitmar to have withdrawn from the route when they did, giving them time to continue establishing *Fairstar* on the Australian cruising scene and *Fairwind* and *Fairsea* in America. With the American travel trade at last working with Sitmar, the line felt secure enough by February, 1973 to transfer *Fairwind* to Port Everglades, from where she operated a series of 7-day cruises into the Caribbean. This was the most fiercely competitive and rapidly expanding area of the cruise business and there was an unprecedented number of ships operating cruises out of Miami and Port Everglades, sixteen in all. Several of these were strikingly new, purpose-built vessels belonging to the aggressive Norwegian cruise lines. Nevertheless, with her elegantly modernised profile and her smart interiors, *Fairwind* quickly became one of the most popular cruise ships in the Caribbean. Her expansive lidos and shady promenades made her ideally suited to cruising in the tropics – so different from the days when she had made those occasional visits to the same waters under the Cunard flag. Meanwhile, *Fairsea* continued to enjoy similar popularity and success on the American West Coast with her summer cruises from San Francisco up to Alaska and her winter cruises to Mexico from Los Angeles.

The reputation of Sitmar Cruises continued to grow. *Fairsea* and *Fairwind* were staffed by dedicated crews and were superbly maintained. The very Italian ambience and the Vlasov Group tradition of service that the owner instilled into the company ensured an unprecedented number of repeat passengers. Both *Fairsea* and *Fairwind* compared very favourably with the new vessels that were then entering service: even those glamorous Norwegians of the Royal Viking Line never provided the same high quality of food and service or even the spacious cabins that Sitmar offered. The Sitmar ships, with their sturdy, deep-draft, North Atlantic hulls and strong bows built to withstand any seas, ensured their passengers a far more comfortable voyage than the new cruise ships could offer. There are many reports of *Fairsea* or *Fairwind* slicing through Pacific waves and passing some much newer ship that was taking a pounding.

Before very long, both *Fairsea* and *Fairwind* were operating longer cruises. Both had already experimented with 17-day trans-Canal cruises and from the very outset Sitmar had promoted the idea of longer cruises by the combination of two itineraries. Now, as well as operating the standard 7-day trips that most of their competitors

A familiar, yet sensational, image of *Fairsea* in Glacier Bay, Alaska. *Author's collection.*

***Fairwind* at anchor off Grand Cayman in 1986.** *Alberto Bisagno.*

seemed to focus on, Sitmar expanded into cruises of 10, 11 and 14 days as well. The spaciousness of the ships made them ideal for these longer voyages, though it would be several years before they sailed beyond the Caribbean, Mexico or Alaska. Even confined to those areas, they offered a huge range of different itineraries, their slightly longer cruises allowing them to call at a wider variety of ports. While both ships moved, on a seasonal basis, into the Caribbean or to Panama Canal transit cruises, it seemed that *Fairsea* was to remain the 'Alaska ship' and each summer found her heading north. Eventually, she made Vancouver rather than San Francisco her base port for her Alaskan voyages. This diversity of cruises, coupled with the overall comfort of the ships and Sitmar's good service, undoubtedly helped give the line its enviable reputation.

Fairwind and *Fairsea,* once outmoded Atlantic liners, had taken Sitmar Cruises to the very pinnacle of success and popularity. By 1975, the company was looking to expand its fleet and briefly considered another former Canadian service liner, the one-time *Empress of Britain.* Over the next few years, various other second-hand vessels were also looked over and Sitmar even went as far as purchasing the redundant former Portuguese liner *Principe Perfeito.* They announced ambitious plans to convert her. However, nothing came of them and in 1980, well over forty years after Sitmar began operations, they decided to order their first-ever purpose-built passenger ship. The contract was signed in October, 1980 with Constructions Navales et Industrielles de la Méditerranée of Toulon for a vessel of 38,000 gross tons. She was to be named *Fairsky,* recalling an old favourite of the fleet that had been withdrawn from service in 1977 after being seriously damaged when hitting an unmarked wreck off Djakarta. In what appeared to be a retrograde step, Sitmar announced that she would be powered by steam turbines, instead of the now more usual diesel engines. Their thinking behind this decision was very simple: the other ships of the fleet were turbine-driven and therefore the Sitmar engineers were already familiar with this kind of machinery.

Although originally scheduled for delivery early in 1983, the new ship would not in fact be handed over to her owners until April, 1984. Various delays in both design work and construction brought about this revised schedule. Sitmar gave a great deal of thought to their new vessel and not least to her public rooms. *Fairwind* and *Fairsea* were undoubtedly her rôle models and her promenade deck boasted a run of public rooms so similar in many ways to the rebuilt Cunarders that it was difficult at first glance to tell them apart. For all her modernity, the new flagship of the Sitmar fleet gave more than just a passing nod to her ocean liner heritage. From her public room arrangement, one could be forgiven for thinking that she was, in fact, a former two-class liner. Her main rooms were flanked by broad promenades and, like her fleetmates, she had two dining rooms. There were differences, of course, one of the main ones being that on the new ship the large forward lounge was configured as a 'show lounge' to cater for the increased demand by cruise passengers for staged entertainment.

With a glittering new flagship in the wings, Sitmar arranged to have her consorts *Fairwind* and *Fairsea* refitted in a similar style. Even without the incentive of the impending arrival of the *Fairsky*, a refurbishment of the two sisters was becoming overdue. By this time, they had been sailing for Sitmar for twelve years and interior décor that had been vibrant and modern in 1972 was looking distinctly dated by 1984.

In fact, the refurbishment of *Fairwind* and *Fairsea* had been planned in conjunction with the designing of the new *Fairsky* so that the three ships could have a fully co-ordinated style. The Genoa-based designer Giacomo Erasmo Mortola, who was responsible for some of the interiors of the new ship, was also given charge of the changes to *Fairwind* and *Fairsea*. The work was done at the shipyard at Norfolk, Virginia and *Fairwind* was the first to undergo the transformation. The process began on the 2nd April and took until the 26th April. Her first cruise sporting her 'new look' departed Port Everglades two days later. *Fairsea* underwent her similar transformation exactly a month later. Both ships had the public rooms along their Promenade Decks completely rebuilt and other rooms were redecorated. At the same time, the cabins were also refurbished.

Sitmar literature published to promote the new look *Fairsea* and *Fairwind* said that the ships "have been remodelled from stem to stern". They had, indeed, undergone a dramatic change, although the overall layout of the rooms on the Promenade Deck was very similar to the original configuration. The Forward Lounge lost its grand lounge/ballroom appearance and now had a high proportion of sofas fixed in a forward-facing position, looking towards a stage. They were supplemented by free-standing chairs, again all arranged to face forward. On the starboard side of this room an entirely new cocktail bar was built, with simple and elegant décor which gave it a distinctly Art Deco feel. What had once been an area of shops was transformed into the Promenade Lounge. An inner promenade was created along the starboard side, flanked on the one hand by shops and on the other by a restyled casino. The Grill and adjacent cocktail bar were turned into a lounge and cocktail bar. The aft-facing lounge remained structurally unchanged, though out on deck twin buffet counters were created under the overhang of the deck above. It was, perhaps, at this moment that the former Cunarders looked their very best. But so they should, as apparently $25 million had been spent on the remodelling of the two ships and they seemed to glow with rich colours, handsome fabrics and exciting modern artworks.

With three ships now serving the American cruise market, there were, of course, some re-arrangements of the itineraries. *Fairsky* was based on the American West Coast to take over the sailings to Mexico and up to Alaska that *Fairsea* had maintained for ten years. *Fairsea* herself was now put on the Los Angeles, Panama Canal, Curaçao route during the winter and then returned to the Mexican cruise itinerary between May and October. *Fairwind* continued to sail out of Port Everglades to Caribbean ports. In 1986, with the increased popularity of cruises to Alaska, *Fairsea* made a return to those northerly waters. But, while *Fairsky* was operating 12-day cruises out of San Francisco, *Fairsea* was based at Seattle and made 10-day cruises. There were further changes at the end of the Alaska season when *Fairsky* replaced *Fairwind* in the Caribbean and *Fairwind* was transferred to the trans-Canal cruises – then running between San Juan and Acapulco. *Fairsea* now maintained a regular series of cruises throughout the winter months from Los Angeles to Mexico. A similar programme was operated during the following year, 1987.

Sitmar had begun further expansion plans for the fleet as soon as *Fairsky* entered service. The Japanese, anxious to prove to the World their ability to build luxury cruise ships, offered a very futuristic design but it seemed as though the deal would be set with the Italian shipbuilding concern Fincantieri. However, there was a disagreement relating to building subsidies and Sitmar withdrew. Further tenders were sought and bids were received from several shipyards around the World. It was on the 26th June, 1986 that Sitmar announced that they would place an order with Chantiers de l'Atlantique of St. Nazaire for a 60,000-ton cruise ship with a passenger capacity of 1,700. An option for a second ship was also signed. Construction was scheduled to begin early the following year and the ship was due to be delivered at the end of 1988.

With this contract signed, Sitmar again turned their thoughts towards even more new tonnage and once again they entered into negotiations with Fincantieri. Eventually, they cancelled their option for a second vessel from Chantiers de l'Atlantique and signed a contract with Fincantieri for two ships. Once operators of second-hand emigrant-carrying liners from diverse backgrounds, they were now thrusting themselves forward with a prestigious fleet of new and highly sophisticated cruise ships. Would there still be a place for the stalwart *Fairwind* and *Fairsea*? Alongside such striking new fleetmates, would they be able to attract a following of their own? As things were to turn out, there was to be a far different scenario from that which anyone could have predicted.

On the 2nd November, 1987, Boris Vlasov died of cancer. He was in Japan, where he had gone for treatment. It was as a result of his guidance that the Vlasov group and Sitmar had prospered. Through his vision, Sitmar Cruises had developed into one of the major players in the cruise industry.

In 1988, in anticipation of their large new cruise ships soon to enter service, Sitmar embarked upon a programme of updating their image. The quiet, discreet look of a

Fairwind during her 25-day refit at the Norfolk Shipbuilding & Engineering Co. yard at Norfolk, Virginia in 1984. *Alberto Bisagno.*

traditional ocean liner operator was to be discarded in favour of something felt to be more suited to a cruise company in the 1980s and 1990s. The buff funnels were to be repainted deep blue and the simple V logo was to be replaced by a stylised swan in white and red. Along a quarter of the hull, toward the stern, there was to be a design of red and blue curving lines, sweeping up into the superstructure and echoing the curves of the swan logo. Sitmar went to great pains to promote this new look. In one of their brochures they stated: "Our contemporary new logo features a swan-shaped 'S' resting on three gentle waves. The new logo beautifully communicates what Sitmar offers. The swan gliding serenely in water symbolises elegance, relaxation. The waves suggest a calm and soothing sea. The effect is a reflection of Sitmar's commitment to quality, the essence of every Sitmar cruise. The new symbol will in time grace the funnels of all Sitmar ships. And the wave in the logo will be prominently displayed on the hull of each ship – making Sitmar the first cruise line to use such an eye-catching graphic in this manner."

The design was, in fact, almost universally derided, especially as a large proportion of the wave logo on the hull would end up being underwater. Another aspect of this rather unfortunate corporate style was the renaming of all the ships. Each was to bear the prefix Sitmar. *Sitmar Fairwind*, for example. As it tuned out, *Fairwind* would be the only ship in the fleet to have the misfortune to suffer this ill thought-out concept.

Apart from a new look, Sitmar also planned to offer a considerably expanded schedule of cruises for 1988. In February, *Fairwind* made the first of two cruises up the Amazon. This must have been one of the most exotic and exciting cruises so far made by a Sitmar ship. It began from San Juan and called at Belem, Santarem, Boca Do Valerio and Manaus, from where passengers were flown home. Meanwhile, another load of passengers was flown into Manaus to join the ship for the return. A similar cruise was undertaken two months later, in April.

During that summer, *Fairwind* developed mechanical problems. During a Mexican Riviera cruise in June, one of her propeller shafts broke. She had to be 'deadheaded' up to a San Francisco shipyard for lengthy repairs. Worse still, with her schedule now totally disrupted, she had to be 'deadheaded' all the way from San Francisco to Port Everglades. It was there, in August, that she was repainted in her 'new-look' livery and given the extended name *Sitmar Fairwind*. She was destined, however, to spend only a few weeks with this new identity. She was hardly into her new schedule of cruises from Port Everglades when further mechanical problems struck and she broke down off Nassau in late August. She then had to 'deadhead' once again, this time up to New York where she underwent a month of repairs at New York Shipyards Inc. (formerly the Todd Shipyards plant) in Brooklyn's Erie Basin. This further repair work meant that her official 'maiden arrival' at New York had to be cancelled.

By this time, Sitmar had already announced an even more ambitious programme for 1989. As well as sailings in their familiar cruising areas such as the Caribbean, trans-Panama Canal, Alaska and Canada, the US-based ships would be going further afield to South America, New England and Canada, the South Pacific and to Europe with calls in both Scandinavia and the Mediterranean. Not only was the programme diverse but there was the opportunity to combine several cruises (without repeating a port) to make what Sitmar were calling a 'Grand Adventure Cruise'. One option would be a 30-day voyage aboard what would by then be *Sitmar Fairsea*, sailing from Sydney on the 24th March to Los Angeles, calling at several of the most beautiful islands in the South Pacific. (This was exactly the route that Sitmar had first envisaged for her.) An even more fabulous cruise was planned for *Sitmar Fairwind*. Sailing from Venice on the 28th September, she was to undertake a 66-day odyssey through the Mediterranean, across the Atlantic and into the familiar waters of the Caribbean, then through the Panama Canal and up the West Coast to San Francisco, over to Honolulu and down to several other Pacific islands before arriving at Sydney in December. There were 25 ports of call in all. As they put it in the brochure: "What more could you ask for!" Sadly, this most exciting of cruise programmes ever devised by Sitmar would never take place under their houseflag.

Back Under British Ownership

It came as quite a shock. Even though there had already been some consolidation in the cruise industry in the past year or so, nothing quite prepared it for the announcement that came on the 28th July, 1988. The Peninsular & Oriental Steam Navigation Company, one of the most famous shipping lines in the World, announced from their London headquarters that they had reached an agreement to acquire the entire share capital of Sitmar Cruises. The price paid was $210 million for the four existing ships, *Sitmar Fairwind, Fairsea, Fairsky* and the Australian-based *Fairstar*, plus the cost of the three newbuildings. The acquisition immediately increased the P&O fleet to ten ships, making it the largest cruise fleet in the World at the time. It was noted that cruise operators had been flooding shipyards with orders for new tonnage – with the notable exception of P&O. The Sitmar ships then under construction had all been ordered before the newbuilding boom had taken off, which meant that they would be 20 to 30% cheaper than the more recent orders placed by other companies. In addition, P&O would also be getting three new ships rather sooner than their competitors.

Indeed, it was speculated that P&O had, in fact, only acquired Sitmar in order to increase their own fleet with those large new ships already being built. It was suggested that they had no real interest in the then operational Sitmar fleet, and certainly not *Sitmar Fairwind, Fairsea* or *Fairstar*. There was speculation regarding the areas of employment of these ships. One of the former Cunarders was expected to be based in Europe and the other to partner *Fairstar* in Australia. It was not doubted that the three new vessels would all serve the American market. All the Sitmar ships were to adopt the identity of the P&O subsidiary, Princess Cruises. Sadly, this would be the end of Sitmar Cruises, except in Australia. There, although P&O was well-known, Sitmar was the dominant operator and *Fairstar* would be marketed under the name P&O-Sitmar. For several years, she continued to carry the new Sitmar Cruises logo on her funnel but minus the sweeping graphic along her hull.

An atmospheric view of *Dawn Princess* at anchor off Monte Carlo in September, 1989. *Clive Harvey.*

***Dawn Princess* (left) and *Fair Princess* together at Los Angeles in October, 1992.** *Peter Knego.*

In September, following the dry-docking in Brooklyn to repair her faulty propeller shaft, *Sitmar Fairwind* arrived at her Manhattan berth, but now she was carrying a new name on her bows, *Dawn Princess.* Her funnel, now thankfully free of the tasteless swan logo, was painted white and carried the marginally more attractive 'Sea Witch' logo of Princess Cruises on its sides. In New York, she boarded passengers for a series of cruises to New England and Canada, with calls at Newport, Bar Harbour, Halifax, Sydney, Quebec and Montreal. It was ironic that her first cruise back under British ownership should return her to the old familiar waters of her days under the Cunard flag.

Fairsea was given the name *Fair Princess.* Although now officially units of the Princess Cruises fleet, both *Dawn Princess* and *Fair Princess* continued to maintain the schedules that had been planned for them by Sitmar Cruises. Thus, the two stately former Cunarders were to be seen in several new ports around the World.

For *Dawn Princess,* her 1989 European programme marked a return to many areas that she had not visited since she was known as *Sylvania.* The programme was divided into four separate itineraries, two in the Mediterranean, one to the Norwegian fjords as far as the North Cape and one calling at the Baltic capitals. The first cruise was one of the Mediterranean trips, departing Lisbon on the 4th May for Barcelona, Monte Carlo, Livorno, Naples, Dubrovnik and Venice. The other Mediterranean itinerary was the same route in reverse, with the exception of a call at Malaga instead of Barcelona. Having made four Mediterranean cruises, *Dawn Princess* headed north and in so doing called at Southampton, on the 3rd July. Her last appearance in the port had been nineteen years earlier, in January 1970, when she had been preparing to leave for Italy and the dramatic rebuild. This time, she remained there until the 6th when she departed for Copenhagen. Her first northern cruise was the one and only trip up to the Norwegian fjords and included calls at Oslo, Stavanger, Bergen, the spectacular Geirangerfjord, Honningsvaag for excursions to the North Cape, Trondheim, Sognefjord and back to Copenhagen. She then turned into the Baltic and made three cruises to the beautiful cities that fringe that sea.

By the 16th September, *Dawn Princess* was back in Lisbon, ready to undertake two more Mediterranean cruises. (I was aboard for that 16th September sailing. *Dawn Princess* had operated until then with her Sitmar-engaged staff but this was their last trip. Their contracts ended the morning after our arrival in Venice. Thus, the cruise had a certain poignancy about it. Also, the service often lacked finesse. There was, without doubt, some unhappiness that Sitmar had been absorbed into the Princess Cruises operation.)

In fact, it seemed that few were happy about the take-over, other than perhaps the senior management of P&O. The Sitmar crews were certainly unhappy at the dissolution of that special Sitmar-Italian family ambience; those loyal Sitmar passengers were certainly unhappy and, perhaps inevitably, claimed that "it all went downhill after P&O got their hands on the line". On the other hand, passengers that had only ever sailed on one of the modern Princess cruise ships were less than enchanted by the older style of the former liners. Crew members who had only served Princess Cruises and were assigned to either *Dawn Princess* or *Fair Princess* certainly had their own opinions as well, looking down on the ships and considering a posting to either one as some form of punishment.

Many of the crew of *Fair Princess* referred to her as 'Fair Bucket', not being overly impressed by her after coming from the likes of *Pacific Princess* or *Island Princess*. Her working conditions were regarded as nothing short of sub-standard. Behind those doors marked 'Crew Only', few changes had been made since the ships entered service in the 1950s. There were still six-berth crew cabins, with the bathroom down the hall. The crew bar was a small nook off the side of the crew mess, reached by a very steep staircase or by an old-fashioned gated lift. Officers' accommodation was somewhat different, being located up on Lido Deck, with their mess on Aloha Deck, one deck below the bridge. Here, in the Officers' Mess, perhaps one might have still felt that the Sitmar houseflag was flying from the masthead. The atmosphere was fairly formal: you had to be in uniform to eat there. The conversation was mostly in Italian, as were the menus and, not surprisingly, the food. Eventually, however, and despite what might be considered their shortcomings, both *Dawn Princess* and *Fair Princess* did become very popular ships within the Princess Cruises fleet, both with crew and passengers.

After the ambitious schedule planned by Sitmar for 1989 was at an end, both *Dawn Princess* and *Fair Princess* were assigned to less exciting itineraries in cruising areas where they had been well-loved and popular – the Caribbean, Mexico and Alaska. While they certainly retained some of their loyal passengers and, indeed, built up an even greater following, it was inevitable that their time under the P&O/Princess flag would be limited. Their hulls and machinery were well over 30 years old and, even in their modernised guise, they could still be considered middle-aged. The Princess fleet, like many others, was poised to expand rapidly. It was unlikely that there would be scope for two ageing dowagers of the sea capable of carrying just several hundred passengers in a fleet of modern purpose-built cruise ships that could accommodate well over a thousand passengers each. Under the circumstances, it was perhaps surprising that Princess retained the pair for as long as they did.

Both ships had begun to experience mechanical problems and as a result *Dawn Princess* had to cut short

Passengers return to *Fair Princess* from a day ashore at Cabo San Lucas, Mexico. *Clive Harvey.*

Public rooms on the *Fair Princess* were slightly remodelled to give a warmer atmosphere. *Peter Knego.*

one of her Alaska cruises in August, 1991. The two sisters were scheduled to make a series of 7- and 10-day cruises from Los Angeles to Mexico through late 1991 and early 1992. Before they were to begin, they were sent for dry-docking and repairs at Portland, Oregon. Once the shipyard workers began the work, they realised that the engine rooms contained asbestos – a not surprising fact given the vintage of the ships. As a result of this discovery, a whole new set of problems emerged. Each area of the ship had to be sealed. Only then could the crews, dressed in special protective clothing, get to work in that section. In this way, the asbestos was removed and replaced by a fibre-glass substitute. However, the new material, while effective, did not have the heat-absorbing qualities of asbestos and after the refit the engine rooms could become very hot. Once the ships re-entered service, this would necessitate 3-hour watches instead of the more usual 4-hour ones. In the meantime, the unanticipated work considerably prolonged the refit and as a result the ships remained at Portland for 96 days. Many of the planned cruises to Mexico had to be cancelled and the schedule could not be commenced until December. All this only added to the speculation about just how much longer the ships would be retained by Princess.

By the following summer, there were reports of plans to sell *Dawn Princess* and Princess Cruises even went so far as to make the statement that "she no longer fits into the company's modern fleet". When the schedule for 1993 was published, it contained no mention of her. There was every expectation that her sale would soon be announced and there were rumours linking her first with Premier Cruises and then with Dolphin Cruise Line. However, later in 1992, soon after that announcement that she no longer fitted into their fleet, Princess Cruises reversed their decision and planned a whole new schedule for her. In the spring, she was to sail from southern California to Mexico and then in the summer she would be based in San Francisco for cruises of 10 days duration up to Alaska. There had even been talk of transferring her to Australia for South Pacific cruises or to British waters to maintain a cruise programme there. However, recession in Britain coupled with the high demand in the Alaskan market

Two different extremes of accommodation aboard *Fair Princess*: the Owner's Suite and a three-berth cabin. *Peter Knego.*

influenced the company to change their mind.

It was to be a short-lived reprieve. *Dawn Princess* was destined not to make those cruises to Alaska. Early in 1993, Princess Cruises announced a further change of plan. They would be withdrawing the ship from service that June, at the end of her series of cruises to Mexico. The company had negotiated the charter of the former *Royal Viking Sky*, then sailing on short cruises in the Baltic for the Birka Line of Finland as *Birka Queen*. A much newer and purpose-built ship, she would, Princess Cruises felt, suit their needs and, more importantly, their image far better than the old former Cunarder. Taking the name *Golden Princess*, the one-time Royal Viking Line vessel would assume the Alaskan cruise schedule from *Dawn Princess* on the 13th June.

***Fair Princess* laid up at Los Angeles in May, 1996 at the end of her Princess Cruises career. The Sea-witch logo on her funnel has been painted over.** *Peter Knego.*

Meanwhile, *Fair Princess* remained as part of the Princess fleet. For some reason, the company had not denounced her as "no longer fitting into the modern fleet". Indeed, quite the reverse, it seemed for a while. In early 1993, Princess Cruises issued a lavish brochure entitled 'Beautiful Ships'. In it, she was described thus: "The intimate *Fair Princess* boasts a charming, private-club atmosphere that makes it easy to meet and mingle and make lasting friends. Walnut-panelled walls, gleaming stainless steel rails, luxuriously thick carpet, butter-soft leather, reflective ceilings, etched glass doors and distinctive artwork all evoke seagoing traditions.... This classic ship is packed from stem to stern with fabulous amenities.... *Fair Princess* is an uncommon delight."

Very shortly after the announcement that *Dawn Princess* would be withdrawn from service came the further statement that she had been sold to Happy Days Shipping, a company affiliated with the Vlasov group of Monte Carlo. So, by some strange twist of fate, *Dawn Princess* would in effect become a Sitmar ship once again. She would not, however, trade as such. It was announced that as from the 18th August, 1993, renamed *Albatros*, she would be under charter to the German tour operator, Phoenix Reisen and would sail as the fleetmate to their other chartered ship, the splendidly striking *Maxim Gorkiy*.

***Fair Princess* at Mazatlan, Mexico, being prepared for a new life as an Australian cruise ship.** *Kevin M. Anthoney.*

Sisters Apart

Albatros

Albatros entered service for her new owners in a stylish livery with a blue/green hull stripe and with her black-topped funnel painted the same shade and bearing the company logo of a white bird across an orange disc. She had been handed over to the Vlasov group by Princess Cruises at San Francisco on the 18th June, 1993. The next day, she sailed for Los Angeles where she was dry-docked and given a complete overhaul by the South West Marine Inc. shipyard. On the 13th July, she left for Lisbon, where some further work was undertaken as she lay alongside the Alcantara Dock. There she took on bunkers and stores and was joined by her new crew members. On completion of the work in Lisbon, she sailed for Bremerhaven.

Her passenger complement had been reduced to 720 – when under the Princess flag, she had been able to accommodate 890. She had 340 crew and her officers were both German and Italian. Phoenix Reisen had announced an extensive cruise programme for their newly-chartered ship. After an initial series of nine cruises out of Bremerhaven, ranging in length from 4 to 18 days, they planned to send her on a 100-day world cruise departing on the 5th January, 1994. *Albatros* sailed from Bremerhaven on the 18th August on her first cruise for Phoenix, to the Norwegian fjords. Later in 1993, between the 27th October and the 30th November, she underwent a further refit, this time at the hands of the T. Mariotti company in Genoa. The work was concentrated on restyling her accommodation to be more suited to the tastes of her German passengers.

While she was usually marketed exclusively to German tourists on cruises to Scandinavia and in the Mediterranean, British passengers were offered "A rare opportunity to cruise aboard the *Albatros*" at the end of 1994. From the 23rd November to the 2nd December, she was chartered by a company called Arena Travel for a cruise from Genoa to Livorno, Palma, Almeria, Cadiz, Lisbon and Vigo, ending in Dover. It was a rare and

Albatros sailing from Southampton, passing the motor yacht _Blue Bird_ which once belonged to the pre-War speed ace Sir Malcolm Campbell. *Clive Harvey.*

special opportunity indeed, with fares for this 10-day cruise as low as £399 in a four-berth cabin and £1,098 in a suite.

Earlier in the year, Phoenix had announced that during the first months of 1995 *Albatros* would again sail on a World cruise – this time an incredible voyage of 144 days calling at 64 ports in 37 different countries on 5 continents. Although she was by now almost 38 years old and was an extremely well-travelled liner, the former Cunarder would during this lengthy odyssey visit parts of the World that even she had not seen before. It most certainly proved to be a memorable trip – but not in a way that the executives at either the Vlasov group offices or those of Phoenix Reisen in Bonn would have wished. *Albatros* sailed from Genoa on the 6th January, 1995. Her route was initially quite familiar, across the Atlantic to the Caribbean, through the Panama Canal and up the West Coast to San Francisco. From there, she sailed over to the Hawaiian islands and down through the South Pacific to Australia, including Tasmania. She then took her passengers up through the exotic locations of South East Asia and on to Japan, Korea, China and Vietnam, followed by a crossing of the Indian Ocean to Colombo, Cochin and Bombay. The final leg of this fabulous journey was to be up the Red Sea, through the Suez Canal and finally arriving back in Genoa on the 30th May. Just eight days from the end of the cruise, at 11 pm on the 22nd May, a near-disaster struck.

The Pelikan Restaurant has hints of Art Deco. *Peter Knego*

Albatros was just 60 miles off Yanbu when a flash fire broke out in the boiler room. While the blaze was very quickly extinguished, the fire fighting operation left the ship partly flooded and the boilers were shut down as a safety precaution. Also, her 565 passengers were sent to their muster stations. *Albatros* was all but powerless as she awaited the arrival of a salvage tug. With only auxiliary power available, the air-conditioning system was not working and, to escape the stifling heat within the ship, the passengers spent their time on the open decks. Meanwhile, the crew were at work, trying to establish the cause of the fire. A Russian tug, *SB-408*, arrived to take charge of the crippled ship early on the 24th and towed her to the port of Jeddah, where they arrived on the following day. While the cruise had so far been spectacular, and the fire was certainly a rather disappointing way for it to end, the passengers' treatment on their arrival in Jeddah was nothing short of remarkable. In fact, it turned out to be an incredibly glamorous conclusion to what had surely already been a fabulous experience. King Fahd of Saudi Arabia treated the passengers as though they were his personal guests. At his expense, they were all accommodated in luxurious hotels, a reception was held in their honour at a leading restaurant during which they were all presented with flowers and specially minted coins commemorating the event. The following day, they were flown home on two chartered flights, also paid for by the King.

Initially, there was some uncertainty as to where the repairs to the ship might be carried out. It seemed as though she might be towed to Bremerhaven, but then various Mediterranean yards seemed more likely options. Eventually, she was taken to Livorno for the initial repair but was then towed to Marseilles, where further work was done and more asbestos was removed. It was not until the 26th July that the work was completed. *Albatros* then resumed her summer schedule with an 18-day cruise to Spitsbergen, departing Bremerhaven on the 29th.

When it had first been announced that the ship would be named *Albatros*, there had been many who had pronounced this to be a most unfortunate choice. There had been references to *The Rhyme of the Ancient Mariner* and the connotations of bad luck associated with the albatross sea bird – despite the fact that the ship had sailed trouble-free for Phoenix Reisen for two years before her unfortunate engine-room fire and would sail for a further two years without incident. Nevertheless, when the next incident finally happened, there were letters to the press about her 'unfortunate name'. In fact, one correspondent went so far as to suggest that maybe none of her accidents would have occurred had she retained the name *Fairwind.*

That next incident certainly ensured that *Albatros* was headline news. In fact, the cruise made the news early on, but only in the modest way that good news stories usually do. On the 7th May, 1997, she had sailed from Bremerhaven on a two week cruise around the British Isles, scheduled to call at Invergordon, Kirkwall, Oban, Belfast, Liverpool, Dublin, Cobh, the Isles of Scilly, Cowes, Tilbury, Amsterdam and then back to Bremerhaven. The call at Liverpool, her former homeport,

***Albatros*'s vintage engine room still looked pristine in 1999.** *Peter Knego.*

was on the 13th May. The last time she had been in the Mersey had been in 1967. Now she made a grand sight anchored opposite the famous Liver Building. As his last duty in office, the Lord Mayor of Liverpool went aboard the ship to welcome her passengers to the port. The event was reported in *The Liverpool Echo*, which referred to *Albatros* as an historic cruise ship and acknowledged her former links with the city. Just three days after being the toast of Liverpool, she made the headlines again – only this time, in a big way.

On the 15th May, while *Albatros* was in Cobh, the weather deteriorated sufficiently to prompt the Master to telephone the agent in the Isles of Scilly, expressing his concern for prospects the following day. If the conditions were as bad in the islands as they were in Cobh, he proposed cancelling the call. Assured by the agent that the weather was good and that the pilot would board the ship to the south of Peninnis Head, leading to St. Mary's Roads, where she was to anchor, the Master decided to sail that evening for the Scillies. It was to be *Albatros*'s first-ever call at the islands and it would be a memorable one.

Early next morning, she was at anchor off St. Mary's Pool harbour and during the day her passengers went ashore. Departure was scheduled for 1500 hours. The pilot had assessed the sea conditions and decided that it was too rough, and with the wind against the tide he considered it inadvisable for him to disembark from the ship off Peninnis Head. At 1445 hours, he discussed the sea conditions with the Master and it was agreed that *Albatros* would follow the pilot's launch out to sea. At 1505 hours, while heading through St. Mary's Sound, the ship shuddered, rolled momentarily to port and then to starboard. She had hit the well-charted North Bartholomew Rock, although at the time that fact was unknown. All the Master did realise was that his ship had hit some submerged object on her starboard side. He ordered hard-a-starboard to prevent the propellers from hitting the object, stopped the engines and ordered the watertight doors to be closed. Following the impact, the bow thruster compartment began to flood and instructions were given to engineers to check all other machinery spaces for flooding or damage. The crew alert alarm was sounded and within minutes all lifeboat and life raft preparation parties had been mustered. The Master informed the authorities of the incident and that *Albatros* would return to the anchorage.

Initial thoughts were that she had hit a submerged container lost overboard from a small ship the previous month. However, an inspection of the hull by a diver later that night found evidence that she had in fact struck rocks and it was suggested that the buoy marking the North Bartholomew Rock had possibly shifted during the recent bad weather. Trinity House were, however, quick to deny this. Although *Albatros* was in no danger, it was obvious that her cruise would have to be aborted. Several fuel oil tanks had been ruptured and her bunkers would obviously have to be removed before she could move on to a port to be repaired. Her 504 passengers remained on board the following day while plans were made to return them home. A chartered ferry took them to Penzance and they were then transferred to London for their journeys on to Germany.

The Vlasov Managing Director, Ettore Bonaventura, was hopeful that the ship would be back in service by the 14th June, missing just two cruises. It was expected that she would need maybe 7 or 8 days in drydock and quotations for the work were already being requested from several European shipyards. However, on the 18th May, as emergency repairs were being made to ensure her seaworthiness, a further inspection by divers discovered that she was more seriously damaged than at first believed and suddenly there was the prospect of a period of three or four weeks in drydock. The divers had found damage to four double bottom tanks, a cofferdam and a number of other tanks, stretching for 40 metres along her side.

Once the passengers had left the ship, her hotel staff was also taken off and the Dutch firm Smit Tak began pumping off 480 tonnes of her bunkers into the coastal tanker *Falmouth Endeavour*. The plan was for *Albatros* to steam under her own power to a shipyard, with a tug in attendance. The contract for the repair was awarded to the A&P Group's Southampton facility. The ship was expected to sail on the 24th May but bad weather delayed her departure by one day. As planned, she sailed under her own power but accompanied by the tug *Anglian Earl*. Arriving at the yard the following afternoon, she was put into drydock. This was a tricky operation, given the extent of her hull damage. Once she was there and the hull inspection had been completed, it was evident that a substantial amount of steelwork would be involved in repairing the hull. The work, which had been expected to take up to four weeks, was now re-assessed as likely to take around six weeks. In the end, it was nearer seven, taking up to the 12th July before it was completed. It had been the most serious accident of her life. What saved her from being a total loss was the additional strength built into the ship to help her withstand the ice of the St. Lawrence River. *Albatros* remained alongside New Docks for two days being made ready to resume her cruising schedule.

Eighteen months after *Albatros* hit the rocks, a report on the incident was published by the Bahamas Maritime Authority. It concluded that she had struck a rock pinnacle after turning too widely to gain the leading line for the passage through St. Mary's Sound. Three contributory factors were singled out: first, the pilot decided that weather conditions did not allow safe disembarkation from his launch and therefore led the ship out of St. Mary's Bay by giving instructions by radio; second, there was insufficient precision in fixing the position of the ship; and the third related to certain aspects of bridge procedure. The report did not confirm the owners' initial claims that a key navigational buoy may have moved, thus contributing to the grounding.

The *Albatros*'s return to service did not mark the end of her problems. She sailed from Bremerhaven on the 19th July for a cruise to Norway and Spitsbergen but shortly after having left port she experienced difficulties with her boilers. She returned to Bremerhaven's Columbus Quay and her passengers remained aboard while the necessary repairs were carried out. She was finally able to depart late the next day.

By this time, Phoenix Reisen had bought *Albatros* from Happy Days Shipping, but there were still occasions when she would be chartered to other operators, in the United

After her grounding off the Scilly Isles in May, 1997, *Albatros* was repaired in the King George V drydock at Southampton.
A & P Shipyards.

Kingdom. After P&O retired their liner *Canberra* from service, her former passengers became the target market of various charter companies that were to use *Albatros* on cruises out of the U.K. On the 1st – 14th December, 1997, she sailed from Dover under charter to Equity Cruises, bound for northern Spain, Portugal, Madeira, the Canaries and Morocco. There were further charters to other British tour operators during 1998. On the 5th July, she left Dover for an 11-night cruise to Norway under a charter to The Cruise Collection, a division of Victoria Travel Service, Ltd. of Birmingham; and on the 10th September she sailed on a Baltic cruise with both British and German passengers. In November, she operated four Mediterranean cruises which were made available to British passengers and further cruises in both the Baltic and the Mediterranean were planned under charter to The Cruise Collection and Arena Travel during 1999.

In July, 1998 a new, U.K.-based company calling themselves Mermaid Shipping announced that they had secured a charter of *Albatros* and that they would operate her on a Millennium round-the-World cruise under the unlikely name of *Mermaid Oasis*. Their target market was the over-50s, and very specifically ex-service personnel. Initially, they aimed to operate four 84-day World cruises each year with an emphasis on ports near the sites of World War II battles. It seemed a rather ill-starred enterprise and within a week of announcing the charter of *Albatros* a further announcement was made saying that they had chartered another vessel instead.

On the 7th November, 1999 *Albatros* departed Genoa for a 100-day world cruise to see in the 21st Century. A further extensive cruise programme followed, principally in Europe, and on the 17th December, 2000 she sailed from Genoa on yet another round-the-World odyssey which, this time, lasted an incredible 130 days. Further underlining their commitment to their ship, Phoenix announced in November, 2000 a further ambitious schedule for *Albatros* through until the middle of 2003. This even included the opportunity for passengers to take part of a world cruise aboard *Albatros* and then transfer to *Maxim Gorkiy* for the remainder of the time. This schedule of far-ranging cruises would take her as far afield as Ilulissat and Sisimiut in Greenland, to Funafuti in Tuvala and Bairiki in Kiribati – literally a world away from the Liverpool to Montreal service of the 1950s.

Fair Princess

In early 1995 came the news that Princess Cruises had agreed to sell *Fair Princess* to what was then the ever-expanding Regency Cruises. Delivery would be made following the completion of her programme of summer cruises to Alaska. Regency Cruises announced that the ship would be renamed *Regent Isle* and, on completion of the Alaska programme, she would sail on the 14th October from San Francisco to Hawaii. After cruising the Hawaiian islands, she would return to the West Coast, to Ensenada in Mexico, and then undertake a series of 2- and 5-day cruises out of Tampa into the Caribbean. The Caribbean itineraries were quickly rethought into something considerably more ambitious – 11-, 13- and 23-day cruises between Acapulco and Montego Bay. In the spring, Regency planned to send the ship across the Atlantic for a series of 14-day eastern Mediterranean and Black Sea cruises. The schedule was planned right up to the end of October, 1996. Even postcards of the ship were printed, albeit retouched pictures of *Fair Princess*.

Regency Cruises had been established in 1984, their first ship being the luxurious former Swedish American Line *Gripsholm*. The new line had rapidly found its niche operating this ship and had expanded, acquiring other famous former liners. By 1995, the fleet boasted the former *Royal Odyssey*, which had begun life as the *Shalom*, which Zim Israel Lines had run in Atlantic service. Others in the fleet were the ship that had once been Holland America's *Statendam*, the former Brazilian *Anna Nery* and a much rebuilt ex-Grace Line ship, originally well-known as the *Santa Rosa*. An associated company owned *Calypso*, a cruise ship conversion of a notable Italian ferry. The *Fair Princess* seemed destined to keep illustrious, if somewhat diverse, company. However, just days before Regency Cruises were due to take delivery of her, a chain of events began that revealed that perhaps there was after all some truth in the rumours that had been circulating within the shipping world – the company was in serious financial difficulties.

Regent Star, the former *Statendam*, collided with the side of the Gatun Locks as she was transiting the Panama Canal on the 7th October. Repairs were made to her damaged hull on arrival in Cristobal but it seemed that Regency's funds were perilously low and there were reports of her food running out and of passengers leaving the ship in mid-cruise. Meanwhile, fleetmates *Regent Spirit* and *Regent Rainbow* were placed under arrest in Cannes and Tampa, respectively. The problems continued to escalate and, in the face of mounting financial pressure, Regency Cruises stopped trading over the weekend of the 28th-29th October. All their current cruises were cut short and all future ones were cancelled, causing turmoil among the crews and leaving passengers stranded.

The company had suffered a lessening demand for its cruises in both Alaska and the Caribbean and at that time there was a great deal of heavy discounting in the industry. Regency, with their already low fares were simply unable to compete. The Greek shipping entrepreneur Antonios Lelakis, the owner of Regency, was also facing problems at home, with both the National Bank of Greece and the Hellenic Industrial Development Bank. They had advanced him $110 million to help finance the conversion of a partially-built ferry into a cruise ship. Neither bank had received any repayment from him since mid-1994. Thus, they were poised to seize his Avlis shipyard in Greece.

The sale of *Fair Princess* to Regency had not been

Her decks crowded with passengers, *Fair Princess* leaves Circular Quay, Sydney on her maiden cruise from the port. *John Treacy.*

finalised at the time of the collapse and even back in late September there had apparently been difficulties in financing the deal. In fact, it was believed that it was attempts to raise sufficient funds to buy *Fair Princess* that ultimately brought about the company's collapse. As a result, P&O/Princess were suddenly stuck with a ship they did not want.

At first, she was sent to a berth at Ensenada while Princess tried to negotiate another sale. It seemed very likely at the time that she was fated to become a casino ship. A Florida-based company, with gambling ship intentions, were said to be very interested in her. Nothing came of the plan and *Fair Princess* was sent to a lay-up berth in Mazatlan. For several months she remained in this Mexican port and in some vague attempt at disguise, her Sea Witch logo was covered in white paint and the O, of the letters P&O, was removed from just below her bridge. Then, toward the end of the summer of 1996, P&O announced that their long-serving and hugely popular Australia-based *Fairstar* was to be withdrawn in January, 1997. Although it had been rumoured on several occasions in the past that either *Fair Princess* or *Dawn Princess* might be transferred to Australia, the announcement that *Fairstar* would in fact be replaced by *Fair Princess* came as something of a surprise. At the time, it was reported that, although an older ship than *Fairstar*, *Fair Princess* had undergone many major refurbishments and was therefore of a better standard. The two ships had, in fact, been launched only one day apart but, while the *Fair Princess* had entered service as the *Carinthia* just six months later, it had taken 14 months for *Fairstar* to be completed as the troopship *Oxfordshire*.

At the time of the announcement, there had been some speculation that *Fair Princess* would be renamed for the Australian market, as she would very obviously no longer be a part of the Princess fleet, or so it seemed. This was reinforced by the advance brochures which clearly showed that she would be sporting the very traditional P&O buff funnel colour – much more suitable than the white funnel and Sea-witch logo of Princess. However, the publicity material also showed that her name would remain unchanged. She was to be a Princess, but with an Australian accent.

In November, 1996 *Golden Princess*, the ship that

Princess Cruises had chartered to replace *Dawn Princess*, was making a series of cruises from Los Angeles down to the Mexican Riviera, evoking those early days of Sitmar's entry into the U.S. cruise market. These voyages were a farewell by *Golden Princess* to the Californian coast, where she had built up a loyal following. Her charter to Princess was at an end and she had been sold by Birka to other owners. It was, therefore, somewhat poetic that during one of these final cruises she should dock at Mazatlan just aft of *Fair Princess*, with the old ship being made ready for her further career under the P&O flag. *Fair Princess* was a hive of activity as she was being prepared for the short voyage up to San Diego's Southwest Marine dockyard. She arrived there the following month and underwent extensive refurbishment and upgrading to meet the new Safety of Life at Sea (SOLAS) requirements that had recently come into force.

On the 31st January, 1997 *Fairstar* returned to Sydney at the end of her final cruise. Quietly berthed at Garden Island, where she had undergone still further refitting work, *Fair Princess* was waiting to take over the role as Australia's 'new' cruise ship. On the 6th February, *Fair Princess* and the now retired *Fairstar* were berthed together and the following day *Fair Princess* sailed on her first cruise out of Sydney, fully booked with 1,050 passengers. P&O issued a Press Release that stated:

"A new era in South Pacific cruising begins today with the maiden cruise from Australia of P&O *Fair Princess*, which succeeds *Fairstar* as Australia's only full-time cruise ship. P&O *Fair Princess* will depart the Darling Harbour cruise terminal at 5pm today, fully booked for a 12-night South Pacific cruise. The vessel's other 31 cruises this year have also attracted very strong bookings..." Managing Director of P&O Holidays, Phil Young, said P&O *Fair Princess* had undergone a major refurbishment in preparation for her new cruising career out of Australia. He said the vessel would offer Australians higher levels of comfort and service under the marketing slogan 'the time of your life'. "Through P&O *Fair Princess*, we will be able to broaden the market.... but at the same time carrying on the *Fairstar* tradition," he said. "Our research has shown that Australian cruise passengers now want that little bit extra and this is exactly what P&O *Fair Princess* will deliver. Strong advance bookings.... indicate that consumers are reacting very positively to a better, more stylish cruise experience.... Even better, P&O *Fair Princess* will be managed by Australians for Australians. This will ensure that the expectations of every passenger will be met."

The Press Release went on to extol the key featrues of the ship and included her "classic liner exterior and excellent sea-keeping qualities suited to the South Seas". It also mentioned that, although the ship had been built in 1956, she was rebuilt as a cruise ship in 1971, serving as part of the world-renowned P&O Princess fleet in North America. (Conveniently, it omitted the role played by Sitmar in the conversion.) However, it also stated that *Fair Princess* had undergone major refurbishments in 1984 and 1989 before the refit just completed at the Australian Defence Industry's Garden Island docks.

It was interesting that throughout the Press Release the ship was referred to as the P&O *Fair Princess* in an attempt to underline the fact that, despite her name, she was not part of the Princess Cruises fleet. It was a pity that, given the desire to ensure that no one would confuse her with the Princess Cruises operation, P&O did not restore her Sitmar name of *Fairsea*, thus ensuring a continuity with the much-loved and recently retired *Fairstar*.

Although the Press Release had attempted to reassure future passengers and although advance bookings were very encouraging, not everyone was happy with the ship. For many, *Fairstar* had been 'their ship' and they were unwilling to accept any other. Many others resented the fact that P&O had –and I quote – "used Australia as a dumping ground for old ladies in their dotage". *Fair Princess* was seen by some as being far too old and lacking in the facilities that today's passengers demand. The layout of her modestly-sized public rooms – as opposed to the larger ones on *Fairstar* – and their sober-toned, mid-1980s Sitmar décor did little to dispel this feeling, even though they had, to some extent, been enlivened by both Princess Cruises and P&O in preparation for this new phase in the ship's career. New carpets and upholstery and the inclusion of some artwork, albeit of questionable taste, did little to impress. Obviously, P&O were going to have a tough job selling *Fair Princess* to the Australians.

Unfortunately, her first cruise from Sydney turned out to be an inauspicious beginning to this new chapter in her already long career. Certainly, it did not help her to win the loyalty of those passengers who were mourning the departure of the *Fairstar* for the scrapyards of India. Nor did it convince those who looked enviously at the glittering new ships based in the Caribbean (no matter how inappropriate they might be for the South Pacific). During that first cruise, a small fire broke out in the casino, there was flooding in one of the restaurants and in some cabins due to burst pipes and there were defective lights, showers and telephones. Despite the extensive overhaul work, many of the problems were undoubtedly a result of the many months of inactivity when *Fair Princess* was laid up in Mexico. On her return to Sydney, her passengers were given a refund of a proportion of their cruise fare and a reduction on any cruise taken within the next two years.

Fair Princess sailed on through 1997 on a programme of cruises very similar to those that had been operated by her predecessor: from the traditional 6-night cruise to Melbourne for the famous Melbourne Cup horse race to 14-nights round New Zealand. She was, however, more usually to be found making her way out towards the islands of Vanuatu, New Caledonia, Fiji and on occasions up to the Solomon Islands and Papua New Guinea. While her itineraries were idyllic, things aboard *Fair Princess* were running far from smoothly, as she was still suffering from mechanical problems. Things came to a head when, during her annual overhaul in February 1998, further defects were revealed. The extensive repair work required

Artwork of questionable quality graced her night club. *Chris Mason.*

resulted in her 11-day cruise to the Loyalty Islands and New Caledonia, due to depart on the 16th February, being cancelled.

The repairs completed, *Fair Princess* was made ready for her next cruise. During the afternoon of the 27th February, her passengers boarded, all looking forward to a 9-night trip, which the brochure called 'Escapist's Dream'. As the hour of her departure neared, the passengers lined her decks, the music played, the streamers were thrown and she began to make her way from the Darling Harbour Cruise Terminal out into Sydney harbour. Then, all four of her generators failed. *Fair Princess* was moved back to the terminal and through the rest of the evening and into the night her engineers worked to get the errant machinery operational again. By the early hours it was evident that the 'Escapist's Dream' would remain just a dream. The cruise would have to be cancelled and her would-be passengers awoke to this bad news.

It just so happened that at *Fair Princess*'s worst hour, the very person who would turn out to be her saviour was in Sydney – none other than the Chairman of the entire P&O group, Lord Sterling. Once he learned of *Fair Princess*'s misfortune he was, by all accounts, immediately on the telephone to America to organise an emergency repair crew. This was made up of Princess Cruises engineers who had worked aboard the ship and were familiar with her machinery. The existing crew had been transferred from *Fairstar* and did not have any significant knowledge of their new ship in order to repair her properly. It must have been with some trepidation she was finally eased away from the cruise terminal on her next scheduled cruise, on the 8th March. However, all went well and the cruise passed without any problems. Nevertheless, P&O were not taking any chances and the repair crew remained onboard until they were happy that all her problems were over. In fact, responsibility for deck and engineering crew was transferred to Princess Cruises and thus *Fair Princess* became a hybrid ship within the P&O empire, being managed by P&O Australia but with a deck crew in Princess Cruises uniforms.

As she continued to sail through her second year out of Sydney, *Fair Princess* began to acquire a following. P&O were making an effort to promote her as a different type of ship offering a more refined and more elegant cruise experience and it was an image that suited this dowager vessel very well. Although her size and sea-keeping qualities made her well-suited to the kind of cruises she was making, with lots of sea-days, rumours continued to circulate that she would soon be replaced. The very ship that Sitmar Line had first had built to their own design, *Fairsky*, at that time sailing as Princess Cruises' *Sky Princess*, was the one most often cited as being her replacement. However, P&O (Holidays) Australia even went so far as to issue a Press release stating: "all the *Sky Princess* rumours, no matter how credible they appear, are untrue". Nevertheless, in April 1999 P&O's Annual Report clearly stated that *Sky Princess* was to be transferred to their Australian cruising operation in November, 2000. She would be the largest and newest ship in the market.

P&O were, in fact, meeting the challenge that had been set by a new operation, Norwegian Capricorn Line, a division of Norwegian Cruise Line, who had transferred their *Norwegian Star*, formerly *Royal Viking Sea*, to Australia. *Sky Princess* would perhaps meet that challenge well, but what of *Fair Princess*? Rumours circulated that she would be sold. Instead, however, P&O continued to change the marketing emphasis of the ship, which they had already begun to put into effect even before the announcement of *Sky Princess*'s planned repositioning. Initially, there had been the move away from the 'fun ship' style that had been exemplified by *Fairstar* – instead, as that Press Release had implied, *Fair Princess* would provide a more elegant and sophisticated cruise experience. However, publicity material for 1999/2000 showed a return to the 'fun ship' style. While the itineraries were the same as before, the brochure was more brash and showed the prices of several of her cruises to be reduced by up to A$500. It gave the impression that P&O were anxious to attract new passengers as well as to hold onto those that had remained loyal for so many years.

In December, 1988 it was announced that a two-week cruise, scheduled to depart Sydney on the 22nd February, 1999 would be cancelled. Instead, *Fair Princess* would undergo a refit to enhance her facilities, in particular those out on deck. It was an inescapable fact that what had been virtually the last word in cruising elegance when the ship first entered service for Sitmar 27 years previously did have some limitations. The often-heard complaint aboard *Fair Princess* was that she did not have enough open deck space. The larger of her two pools, down on Promenade Deck, was usually surrounded by plastic patio furniture, as this area acted as the alfresco dining space, the lunch buffet being served from two curving counters just under the overhang of the deck above. As most of the passengers seemed to like the outdoor life and just about all of *Fair Princess*'s cruising was done in tropical conditions, this space for serving food and for eating it was very limited. It should be borne in mind that the ship was often sailing with 1,000 passengers.

Fair Princess returned to Sydney on the 15th February after a 14-night cruise around New Zealand and then went straight to the shipyard to undergo the work that would change not only her outdoor spaces but also some of the public room arrangements. The Scuba Diving Hut was removed from the Lido Deck and was replaced by an 'outdoor food outlet' selling pies and pasties. Called Harry's Café de Waves, it was to be operated by a company who had a similar, land-based café at Woolloomooloo. A temporary cover was made for the Promenade Deck pool so that it could be utilised as a dance floor in the evenings, giving the opportunity to provide an outdoor disco into the early hours of the morning. A retractable awning was installed for use in the event of a sudden tropical downpour. In the restaurants, many tables were made larger, to accommodate parties of 8 or 10. Sadly, the gaming tables were removed from the casino into what had been the most elegant area of the ship, Harry's Bar, and a door was installed between the two rooms, thus in effect enlarging the casino facility. Even though the larger *Sky Princess* was due within 18 months, the refit underlined P&O's obvious intention of attracting to the *Fair Princess* those former *Fairstar* passengers who had hitherto been reluctant to accept her.

However, despite all the optimism from the company, in July 1999 the glare of bad publicity was again on *Fair Princess*. The Australian health authorities issued an urgent warning to hundreds of her passengers after an outbreak of typhoid fever. Three passengers who had been aboard the ship for a cruise to Papua New Guinea and the Solomon Islands in May had contracted the disease. Further bad publicity came after several students behaved in a riotous manner when they were aboard the ship for an 'end-of-year schoolies cruise'.

Fortunately, *Fair Princess* rose above these minor problems and appeared to be facing a very bright future, despite the continued rumours that she would be sold off. The refitting and restyling of the ship appeared to be very popular with the passengers and the majority of them were reported as saying that they were keen to sail on her again. Indeed, such was the ship's popularity that one survey reported her as being "By far Australia's most popular cruise ship". To be fair, there was not a great deal of competition – only the *Norwegian Star*, and she had got off to a somewhat shaky start to her Australian-based cruise programme. P&O's General Marketing Manager, Suzie Drinkwater, confirmed that the 'fun-ship' style of cruise was well-established aboard *Fair Princess*. "The improvements we have made on board *Fair Princess* this year have clearly won the approval of our passengers who are having more fun than ever and wanting to do it all again. Almost all our cruises are departing fully booked so 1999 is shaping up as an excellent year." The company also stated that the ship would undergo further refitting work later in the year.

For a while, it had seemed that *Fair Princess* would sail alongside the newly introduced *Pacific Sky* (as *Sky Princess* was to be renamed) out of Sydney. However, by the end of 1999 it was evident that P&O had more ambitious plans in mind for her. It was announced that when *Pacific Sky* began her cruises out of Sydney, in November 2000, *Fair Princess* would be repositioned in Auckland. Some cruises would take her further into the Pacific, to such exotic locations as Tonga, Fiji and Samoa. The positioning of the ship in New Zealand was hailed as being innovative and

Her old-style promenade decks made *Fair Princess* an ideal ship for tropical cruising. *Clive Harvey.*

exciting. The published cruise schedule showed the last cruise of the series, more of a line voyage in fact, departing Auckland on the 5th March, 2001 and arriving back in Sydney on the 9th March. This brief voyage back to Sydney seemed somewhat final at the time, as nothing was projected beyond that date. However, despite any misgivings that anyone might have had regarding the future of *Fair Princess*, the sudden announcement by P&O on the 19th June, 2000 came as a shock:

"Cancellation of *Fair Princess* Auckland/Auckland Cruise Programme.

"We very much regret to announce that we need to cancel the complete *Fair Princess* Auckland/Auckland cruise programme.

"For your information, P&O Cruises has negotiated the sale of *Fair Princess* earlier than anticipated to an offshore buyer and the terms of the purchase mean that the ship must leave our fleet. P&O Cruises had initially intended the sale delivery date for *Fair Princess* to be at the end of her New Zealand programme. W`e are extremely disappointed and apologise that these cruises cannot proceed. We believe that there is a lot of support for future cruises out of New Zealand and in time we will be further exploring these opportunities."

So, the rumours had all been true. However, the following day the saga took another interesting twist when it was revealed just who was behind the purchase of the ship. A Press Release was issued by a company called the Great Canadian Gaming Corporation. It stated that:

"The Company is pleased to announce that it has entered into an agreement to acquire a 25% interest in a cruise ship known as the tss *Fair Princess*. This cruise ship is 175 metres in length and measures 24,800 gt, has 475 cabins and can carry over 1,000 passengers and over 400 officers and crew. The purchase price will be US$15,500,000, of which US$3,875,000 is the Company's portion. Closing is scheduled in the next 30 to 90 days. The ship is presently in dry-dock maintenance to maintain class and will be chartered back to P&O Holidays Ltd. UK on closing until the beginning of December 2000 when it will be delivered to Hong Kong to be refurbished, upgraded and reconfigured for an additional expenditure of up to US$5,000,000. In addition to its 25% interest in the ship, the Company will manage the casino and entertainment operations. The ship will be based in the South China Sea to service the medium and short haul cruise ship and entertainment market."

On the 7th September, the Allegiance Capital

Looking immaculate and with her name in Chinese lettering on her stern quarter, *China Sea Discovery* lies at anchor at Hong Kong, awaiting employment. *Johan Van Delden. Jonathan Boonzaier collection.*

Corporation, a Dallas-based investment banking firm, announced its negotiated purchase of *Fair Princess*, stating that she would be converted into a five-star luxury casino. The participants in the venture were announced as being Great Canadian Casinos and Lake City Casinos in Vancouver and a Hong Kong-based investor in the travel and tour business. "This transaction was a big gamble that has paid off handsomely," explained David Mahmood, the president and founder of Allegiance Capital. "The revenue stream that Allegiance will share is expected to generate several millions of dollars in annual profit. The ship will be ready before the Chinese New Year and we project annual revenue to be in excess of $100 million for the first year alone." Then he made a statement that would seem to be totally alien to the more genteel days in which the former *Carinthia* was built: "This deal was highly unique in that I never left my office here in Dallas. Of course, we had someone examine the vessel, but all negotiations and the transaction itself were handled via e-mail, phone and fax and were completed in less than 90 days." It was also revealed that the ship would be renamed *Emerald Fortune* and that her cruises would be of 2, 3 and 4 days duration.

So, it seemed that the venerable *Fair Princess* would undergo some transformation into a cruise ship aimed at the gambling fraternity. Given the dominance in South East Asian waters of the vast, new and purpose-built cruise ships of Star Cruises, most of which had been created with lavish gaming facilities, to consider moving a rather more modestly-sized, almost 50 year old former trans-Atlantic liner into the area was in itself a gamble.

Fair Princess's final months of cruising under the P&O flag were not to be without incident. In early September, four passengers were taken off the ship and admitted to a hospital in Noumea, New Caledonia, after being diagnosed as having pneumonia. Several other passengers were reported to be suffering from 'flu-like symptoms and there were rumours of a 'legionella virus' aboard. Nevertheless, *Fair Princess* received a clean bill of health by the time she arrived back in Sydney to take up duty as an hotel ship, along with several other cruise ships from all over the World, to provide accommodation for the Olympic Games that were held there. Once the Games were over, *Fair Princess* had less than two months left as a Sydney-based cruise ship. During her last cruises, engineers from the ship management company V. Ships were aboard, indicating that the company would be providing staff and crew for the management and operation of the ship during her new career.

After a somewhat shaky start, *Fair Princess* had established a good following among the Australian and New Zealand cruising public. However, she did not win the hearts of everyone. Some friends of Australian ship enthusiast Stephen P. Moore, who were accustomed to rather higher class ships, uncaringly referred to her as 'Fair Bucket' – the same derogatory name used for her by some of the Princess Cruises people during her early days with that company. Nevertheless, Stephen's response is an appropriate way to close this chapter of the ship's life: "She wasn't that flash, but she wasn't that bad either, and during her time in Australian waters she almost always sailed full."

She would not be sailing full, however, in the coming months. She slipped out of Sydney harbour virtually unnoticed on the 15th November, 2000, a few days after she had finished her last cruise. Before leaving, she was de-stored by P&O and some of her small artwork collection was transferred to *Pacific Sky*. New carpets were delivered and appear to have been fitted before her departure – a curious fact when one considers that extensive refitting and up-grading was planned for her. She arrived in Hong Kong on the 29th November for further work to be done on her.

In February, 2001 it was reported that her name had been changed from *Emerald Fortune* to *China Sea Discovery*. It was said that many of the Hong Kong-based gambling ships have their names changed quite regularly because of the superstitious natures of the gamblers aboard. Apparently, she was now owned by a company called China Sea Cruises, although initially Emerald Cruises had been quoted as the name of her owners. China Sea Cruises had hoped to break fresh ground with an ambitiously planned programme of cruises aimed at the potentially huge Chinese market, sailing between Hainan

Island and Vietnam. However, these plans came to a halt when it was realised that the ship's draught was too deep for the Hainan harbour of Haikou. China Sea Cruises transferred her to the overnight gambling run from Hong Kong. She was far from successful, being reported as often carrying as few as 20 passengers/gamblers. The one-time pride of the Cunard Line had fallen upon hard times indeed and even her owner, a Mr. Robert Ming, was reported as being disgusted by the behaviour of the casino clientele. There were fights, with even the stewardesses being punched, and cabins were stripped of everything moveable, from curtains and bed sheets to toilet rolls.

It was not until April that negotiations were completed for an alternative, deeper berth to be allocated to the ship at Hainan and the planned cruises could begin. It seemed at last that *China Sea Discovery* could settle into a regular and interesting cruise service, and her owners were rumoured to be considering basing her in Taiwan for the summer season. She still looked magnificent: her black-topped funnel was now scarlet with a pale blue and white diamond design on it, her hull still carried the broad blue sheer line and, while her name and port of registry were spelled out in English, they also appeared in Chinese script on her stern quarter.

The Hainan cruise venture turned out to be very short-lived. Pacific Cruises (Hainan), who were by now operating China Sea Discovery, announced at the end of April that they had bought an 11,000-ton luxury ferry, *N. Kazantzakis*, from the Greek company Minoan Lines and planned to convert her into a cruise ship. *China Sea Discovery*'s deep draft and high fuel consumption had apparently persuaded them to bring their charter of the ship to an end, even though they were not expecting the conversion of their new vessel to be completed for several months.

By June, *China Sea Discovery* was laid up in Kaohsiung, Taiwan, while China Sea Cruises began to formulate another plan that would enable them to break into the Asian cruise market. Rumours circulated regarding the future of the ship: one report was that she would be renamed *Lanzhuanshi* and would operate for the Chinese travel company Tropical Island International; another indicated that she was to be put under charter to Phoenix Reisen and would sail alongside her sister *Albatros*. The Managing Director of Phoenix Reisen, when questioned about this, rather pointedly denied the rumour, saying, "One *Albatros* is enough for us." Then there were further reports that she had been sold to Indian breakers, that she was on her way to the Mediterranean and then, perhaps more believably, that she would be operating cruises out of Taiwan. This, indeed, turned out to be the case. On the 12th June, this time sporting blue funnel colours, *China Sea Discovery* departed Kaohsiung on her first cruise from that port.

As this is written, *China Sea Discovery* remains in this service. Her cruises make a brief call at Laok in the Philippines, for what is described as 'technical reasons'. In fact, Taiwanese law states that she must call at a foreign port before returning to Taiwan. This short call does not allow passengers to go ashore. It remains to be seen how successful this new phase in the ship's career will be, but photographs show her still looking splendid.

A brochure in English and Chinese, published in Hong Kong, advertises the attractions of *China Sea Discovery*. *Jonathan Boonzaier collection.*

Sisters Into The 21st Century

The decision by Cunard to build *Saxonia* and *Ivernia* was a bold expression of their faith in the continuance of the Atlantic service. It was perhaps short-sighted of them not to have appreciated the real impact the airlines would make and thus specify a design for much more of a dual role as both liner and cruise ship. The further decision to follow up the original sisters with an almost identical pair was a further poorly thought-out move. By the time those ships, *Carinthia* and *Sylvania*, entered service, the airlines were certainly beginning to take the lucrative business traffic on the Atlantic run, if not the tourist trade. While it is easy to be wise with hindsight, it has to be said that all the indications were already there that times were changing for the Atlantic liners. However, Cunard remained firm in their belief that there would always be those who preferred to travel by sea rather than by air. How true. Nevertheless, they were insufficient in numbers to ensure year-round, and thus long-term, profitability for the Saxonia sisters – and the other liners, not only in the Cunard fleet.

We must be grateful to Cunard, however. Despite their dated designs, the Saxonia sisters were very significant ships in that great renaissance of shipbuilding that took place in the years following the Second World War, symbolic of a return to peace and prosperity. They were part of the mighty Cunard Line fleet when it was at its absolute zenith, achieving everything that Samuel Cunard could have envisaged. It was sad that the decline should have been so rapid and that the Saxonia sisters should have played a part in that decline. Nevertheless, the four handsome ships have served all their owners well, in operations ranging from 3-night cruises to nowhere to world cruises of 144 days.

As 'Finished with Engines' was rung up on the former *Saxonia* when she arrived at an Indian ship-breaking yard, her sister, once the *Ivernia*, remained in lay-up, awaiting a similar fate. Meanwhile, *Carinthia*, as *China Sea Discovery*, and *Sylvania*, as *Albatros*, continued to sail on. Loved by their crews despite their lack of modern, so-called glamour, and loved also by most of their passengers – it is noted by many that these ships have a way of seducing you with their unexpected charm. As they enter the 21st century, both are remarkably well-maintained and belie their 40+ years.

The ultimate success of all four of the Saxonia sisters is a tribute to their designers and builders at the John Brown shipyard. *Albatros* and *China Sea Discovery* are also a tribute not only to Boris Vlasov for his vision, but to all those at Sitmar and the Arsenale Triestino – San Marco yard who were responsible for what turned out to be a most remarkable conversion of two conventional liners into elegant and, most importantly, successful cruise ships.

As the century that gave birth to the ocean liner came to a close, the shipyards of Europe were full with orders for cruise ships. They would be larger and more fabulous in the facilities they offered than even the most famous of trans-Atlantic liners of the past. However, none are likely to have careers as long, diverse or successful as the Saxonia sisters.

A nostalgic final look at a splendid class of liners. *A. Ernest Glen, Bruce Peter collection.*

Bibliography

Eliseo, Maurizio: *The Sitmar Liners & the V. Ships*, Carmania Press, London.
Kludas, Arnold: *Great Passenger Ships of the World*, Patrick Stephens, Ltd., Sparkford and Koehlers Verlagsgesellschaft mbH, Herford.
Miller, William H.: *The Last Atlantic Liners*, Conway Maritime Press, Ltd., London.
McCart, Neil: *Atlantic Liners of the Cunard Line*, Patrick Stephens, Ltd., Sparkford.

Architect and Building News.
Architectural Review, The.
Cabinet Maker and Complete House Furnisher, The.
Cruising News.
Daily Mail, The.
Daily Mirror.
Daily Telegraph, The.
Engineer, The.
Evening Times.
Fairplay.
Glasgow Herald.
Greenock Telegraph, The.
Journal of Commerce, The.
Liverpool Daily Post.
Liverpool Echo.
Lloyd's List.
Marine Engineer and Naval Architect.
Sea Lines, the magazine of the Ocean Liner Society.
Shipbuilder and Marine Engine Builder.
Shipping World, The.
Shipping World and Shipbuilder.
Ships Monthly.
Steamboat Bill, the journal of The Steamship Historical Society of America.
Surveyor, journal of The American Bureau of Shipping.
Syren and Shipping Illustrated, The.
Via Port of New York.

Acknowledgements

A great many people have been extraordinarily helpful, generous and kind to me during the time I have been writing this book, sharing with me anecdotes, photographs, publicity material and information.

I am especially grateful to Anthony Cooke of Carmania Press for accepting the project and for his encouragement and enthusiasm for it.

My heartfelt thanks must go to Captain Ron Warwick for his loan of so much valuable material from his own collection. Without his help I doubt whether there would have been a book at all. I must also thank Alberto Bisagno for the loan of publicity material, for being a wealth of information and for his overall enthusiasm for the Sitmar liners. He helped keep me inspired. Very special thanks must also go to Peter Knego for sending me his report on his visits to the laid-up *Leonid Sobinov* and *Fedor Shalyapin,* along with fine photographs of these sisters in decay. Thanks also to Arthur Crook, whose involvement in the conversion of the staid Cunarders into stylish Sitmar ships, made him an invaluable source of information. Thank you, too, to John Adams, Kevin M. Anthoney, Mark Cornford, Luís Miguel Correia, Timothy Dacey, Laurence Dunn, Alan Kittridge, Peter Kohler, Chris Mason, Bruce Peter, Donald Stoltenberg and John Treacy for the use of their photographs; and to Tony Hill for providing essential information; to Stephen P. Moore in Australia for keeping me up-to-date on the career of *Fair Princess*; and to Jonathan Boonzaier in Singapore for doing the same when she became *China Sea Discovery*.

Finally, my thanks go to all my friends for continually asking, "How's the book coming along?" and ensuring that I remained focussed on the task.

Index